Papa

A memoir of a hero and a mentor for the
illegal displaced people, Rev. Dr. Saw Simon

NAW HSAR KA NYAW HTOO "NINA" SIMON

PAPA
A MEMOIR OF A HERO AND A MENTOR FOR THE
ILLEGAL DISPLACED PEOPLE, REV. DR. SAW SIMON

iUniverse books may be ordered through booksellers or by contacting:

iUniverse
1663 Liberty Drive
Bloomington, IN 47403
www.iuniverse.com
1-800-Authors (1-800-288-4677)

Because of the dynamic nature of the Internet, any web addresses or links contained in this book may have changed since publication and may no longer be valid. The views expressed in this work are solely those of the author and do not necessarily reflect the views of the publisher, and the publisher hereby disclaims any responsibility for them.

Any people depicted in stock imagery provided by Getty Images are models, and such images are being used for illustrative purposes only. Certain stock imagery © Getty Images.

Scripture quotations marked GNT are taken from the Good News Translation — Second Edition. Copyright © 1992 by American Bible Society. Used by permission. All rights reserved.

ISBN: 978-1-5320-8220-7 (sc)
ISBN: 978-1-5320-8219-1 (e)

Library of Congress Control Number: 2019913506

Print information available on the last page.

iUniverse rev. date: 03/10/2020

Papa is dedicated to my late father, Rev. Dr. Saw Simon,
my mother, Thramu Naw Tablut Htoo,
my sisters, Thaw Simon and Paw Simon, brothers-in-law
Blut Soe and Marner Po, and my niece, Bluthaw Soe,
my sister-in-law Paw Krit and, my stillborn son Saw Sausau Simon.
Thank God the Father, the Son, and the Holy Spirit.
Thank you Kaw Thoo Lei Karen Baptist Churches
for trusting me with this memoir.
Thank you Kaw Thoo Lei Karen Bapitst Bible School and College.
Thank you Dr. Daniel Age and Dr. Shirley Worland
for reading and helping with my manuscripts.
Thank you my dear family.
Thank you my dear husband, Saw Kay Nay Ywa.

Tribute to Rev Dr Simon by Rev. Alan Marr
Werribee Baptist Church
8th August 2015

"Here is my servant, whom I strengthen —
'the one I have chosen, with whom I am pleased. I have filled him
with my Spirit, and he will bring justice to every nation.
He will not shout or raise his voice or make loud speeches in the streets.
He will not break off a bent reed nor put out a flickering
lamp. He will bring lasting justice to all.
He will not lose hope or courage; he will establish justice on
the earth. Distant lands eagerly wait for his teaching."
Isaiah 42:1-4

I met Rev Dr Simon on 10th October 1994. Frank and Rachel Jackson had agreed to join me on an adventure, which led us to the Kawthoolei Karen Baptist Bible School in the Maela Camp. The students and staff of the Bible School have held an important place in our lives ever since.

One thing I had personally hoped for on this adventure was to spend time with a person who would teach me more about what it means to follow Jesus. Simon was that person. He has been a friend and inspiration since that first day when he first took me down to the stream to teach me how to take a bath.

I am extremely grateful to God for having known him and feel privileged to share with you some of my gratitude with you today

In my many visits to Maela, Simon would meet with me at the beginning and end of most days and we would talk about my life in Australia, and his life and especially the story of the Karen people's struggle.

I picked up very quickly that his love for his people was not a shallow thing. It was deep and he had committed himself to live sacrificially in service of the Karen people. He had given up a promising academic career in Rangoon to intentionally join a refugee community and commit his life to them.

I also know that he was offered many opportunities to leave the border area but he would not do so if it meant that he would not be able to return home to Maela.

Despite the difficult circumstances at Maela he remained in touch with the world He was a regular listener to BBC World Service and would keep me up to date with what was happening around the world.

I am grateful for his visionary leadership. He was always looking for ways to enhance and develop the life and ministry of the Bible School. It is no accident that the Bible School has grown to be one of the largest Baptist seminaries in Asia Pacific region.

He was keen to see leaders develop and grow. It was difficult for foreign teachers to reside in the camp, so, along with Wati Aier of Oriental Theological Seminary in Nagaland, we worked together to bring teachers into the Bible school. For many years OTS graduates have taught the BTS class. In order to help the Bible School become self reliant, we then negotiated for some Bible School graduates to attend OTS in order for them to return and provide leadership. A number of these students have become leaders among the Karens, not only in the border area but throughout the world.

I am grateful for Simon's resilience and ability to see thing in a positive light. He trusted God even when times were difficult. He led the Bible School through floods, fires and even invasions from Burmese troops. In these difficult times he was a faithful leader —a non-anxious presence. In recent years the Bible school has relinquished many staff, as refugees were able to leave for other parts of the world. This created something of a leadership vacuum for those remained behind in the camp but rather than complain Simon saw this as part of God's plan to enable the gospel to spread throughout the world. He was an instrumental figure in the establishment of the Global Karen Baptist Fellowship.

He believed that the spread of Karen people throughout the world would make the world a better place. I agree with him.

He was a man of peace. In 2000, the Baptist World Alliance recognized his commitment to peace and justice by awarding him the BWA Human Rights Award.

He was a shy man, sometimes reclusive and difficult to know but he was always a generous and respectful host.

He had a wonderful sense of humour with a very infectious laugh. He would remember things we laughed about on previous visits and revisit them. He would always remind me of the time I tried to convince him to drink black coffee.

I will always remember his love for his family –Tablut Htoo his beloved wife, who shared all of Simon's ministry with him. His three daughters, Nyawthawpaw as he used to call them, were the light of his life. He was a loving father and very proud of their achievements.

His home was also always overflowing with children who had no families to support them. Each day in Simon's home began and ended with sound of children singing as Simon led them in devotions. That is one of my loveliest memories of Maela.

As the years have passed my respect for him has grown. I will miss him greatly but will always be grateful to God for a life lived for him.

I recently read some words about another Christian man who led a similar life to Simon….

….he did what he did because he wanted to be with Jesus,
in the sense of imitating Jesus' example and obeying his
words. ….. He wanted to be close to Jesus, a loving disciple who
put his feet in Jesus' footprints with stubborn devotion.

Alan Marr

Foreword

Dr. San C Po, revered Karen leader who held positions in both the Karen Baptist Convention and the Karen National Association in the first half of last century wrote,

> "To gauge the present-day attitude and social status of a nation, a knowledge of past history is essential. The past not only makes the present more easily comprehensible, but also enables one to conjecture what the future may hold in store" (1928: 1).

Hence, in this Foreward to the biography of Rev. Dr. Simon's life and work, I seek to lay the foundation of the essence of the values that underpinned his identity as a Christian Baptist Karen, committed to serving his people, oppressed and displaced through decades of war and persecution[1].

The traditions of the Karen clearly indicate that they have not always lived in their present homelands of Burma and Thailand. One legend is that of 'Htaw Meh Pa', the mythical founder of the Karen race who lived with his numerous families in an unknown land to the north, thought to be Mongolia. Soon their country became overpopulated, so led by Htaw Meh Pa, they set out to seek a new and better land. They traveled together until they came to a land called in Karen "Htee Hset Meh Ywa", thought to be

---

[1] This Preface is compiled from excerpts from my doctoral and subsequent research drawn from many sources. For further reading, please refer to Mason (1861); Smeaton (1887); Thanybah (1917; 1904); Marshall (1922); San C Po (1928); Aung Hla (1932); Morrison (1947); Gravers (1999); Cheesman (2002); Rogers (2004); South (2008); Rajah (2008, 2002); Worland (2017, 2015, 2013, 2010); South and Lall (2018).

where the Yang-tse-Kiang River begins in the Gobi Desert. From there, they migrated southwards to become the first people group of Burma, settling in the central lowlands around the Irrawaddy and Sittaung Basins more than 2,700 years ago.

Traditionally, the Karen are farmers and the fertile land of the lowlands was ideal for agriculture. They settled in village clusters with local leaders and an emphasis on the values of kinship. There are seven main sub-groups of Karen who settled in Burma, the majority being S'gaw and Pwo, each with their own language. Their religion was animist and monotheistic – a belief in the ancestral spirits and one creator God, pronounced Y'wa in both S'gaw and Pwo Karen languages. Karen historian Saw Aung La (1932) records:

> "We began to peacefully clear and till our land free from all hindrances. Our labors were fruitful, and we were very happy with our lot. So, we named the land 'Kawlah', a green land free of all evils, famine, misery and strife; a pleasant, plentiful and peaceful country. Here we lived simple, uneventful and peaceful lives, until the advent of the Burman".

Today, the Karen are a multi-religious people, the majority group being Buddhist and Animist with only about 20-30 percent Christian in Myanmar and less in Thailand. Within the Christian belief, different missionization programs have resulted in different affiliations to Catholic and Protestant church bodies. Further, within Protestant, different denomination's mission programs have resulted in Protestant Christian Karen belonging to Baptist, Anglican, Seventh Day Adventist and Pentecostal churches with the majority in both Myanmar, Thailand and those living now in third countries, identifying as Christian Baptist.

As many indigenous people, the Karen have a rich legacy of oral history told in the form of 'hta's which are seven syllable couplets where the last word of each couplet rhymes. The early Baptist missionaries became enthralled in these 'hta's', generating the idea that the Karen were one of the lost tribes of Israel. Especially the 'hta' that tells the story of how the Karen lost their golden book of knowledge, was a vehicle by which those early missionaries won many converts.

> Y'wa gave his children, amongst who were the Karen, golden books of knowledge. However, the Karen lost their book through carelessness and it was eaten by termites. They were then subjected to a wretched existence, ignorant and cruelly oppressed by the Burmans. One of the books was taken by a white brother across the sea and Y'wa promised the Karen that this white man would return with the book one day and that if the Karen people would receive and obey the teachings of the book, they would enjoy salvation and untold blessings.

In the biography written by Rev. Francis Mason (1861) of the first Christian Baptist convert, Ko Tha Byu, the account is told of how this man was given to American Baptist missionary Rev. Adoriram Judson as a servant who connected his people's ancient legend of the white brother and the lost book to this white missionary and the others living in the house and their Bible; thus becoming the first Karen Christian in 1828. Ko Tha Byu became known as "The Karen Apostle" as he and the Western missionaries travelled far and wide across lower and Eastern Burma where whole Karen villages converted from their Animist and Buddhist beliefs to Christianity, thus laying the foundation for the building up of the Baptist Christian church amongst the Karen.

In the early Baptist missionization period in Burma, wherever sizable converts were made, the missionaries built a church which doubled as a school. By 1832, just four years after Ko Tha Byu's conversion, Rev. Jonathan Wade created a written S'gaw Karen script based on Burmese letters, and readers, Bible stories, hymnbook and a Karen thesaurus and dictionary still in use in some schools today were printed and distributed to all these churches. The whole Bible was translated into S'gaw Karen by Rev. Francis Mason with the assistance of one of his early converts Saw Quala in 1853, and into Pwo Karen in 1878.

Christian Baptist Karen who had never had a written script or attended school were interpreting this access to education and the opportunities it afforded them as the fulfilment of the prophecy of their ancient legend of the lost book. They revered their white missionaries as "their paramount chief" and their pastors as "local chief". It seemed a natural progression therefore that these smaller churches in the different areas would band together to provide larger training seminars and conferences which is how the first Karen Baptist Church Area Association was formed in 1840. These Karen Baptist Christians were rapidly developing their spiritual and religious capital into a very effective network with newfound education and resources. In subsequent years, 11 more Area Associations were formed, and in 1913, they joined together to form the Karen Baptist Convention under the wider umbrella of the Burma Baptist Convention.

Concurrent to the American missionization of the Karen in Burma in the 1820s, Upper Burma had been colonized by the British. However, it would take another two Anglo-Burmese wars before the Burman kingdom was deposed and Burma formally annexed to British India in 1886. Even though King Thibaw had officially been deposed in 1885 and sent to exile in India, the British were not able to eradicate rebellion in the Lower Burma, not having enough manpower to quell the rebellion and gain total control of the country in real terms.

By this time, educated Christian Baptist Karen had vision that extended beyond trans-local membership of the Christian church. This led to the creation of a new Karen word – 'dawkelu' – in 1881 when an elite group led by Dr. T. Thanbyah formed the Karen National Association (KNA). The 'dawkelu' translates in English as 'the entire race' and the central purpose of the creation of the KNA was to promote a united Karen identity.

With the Christian Baptist and national networks well established, American missionaries under the banner of the newly formed KNA negotiated with British ruling powers to provide arms to their Karen converts who were very instrumental in their own military campaign under the command of American missionary, Rev. Dr. Vinton to achieve the total defeat the King Thibaw's army in the Lower Burma in January 1886.

Over the following decades leading up to World War II, Christian Baptist Karen became prominent in rank and file as well as non-commissioned and even junior officers in the British Army in Burma. Many retreated with their battalions to India when the British were forced back in the Japanese invasion in 1942 and were instrumental in leading the push back in 1945. Hundreds more of ordinary Christian Baptist Karen villagers formed a resistance army inside Burma under the command of British officer Major Seagram who remained behind. Suffering terrible atrocities from both the Japanese and the newly formed Burma Independence Army, nevertheless, they also played a significant role in helping the British defeat the Japanese and regain their colonial power in Burma, albeit, only for a short few years before Britain granted independence to a Burman majority government in 1948.

In the immediate post-war years, KNA underwent a name change to the Karen Central Organization (KCO) – to better represent the aims of its Karen leaders to form a separate Karen country instead of joining the proposed Union of Burma once independence was granted. This did not happen and while it remains a contentious issue for many Karen, historians and researchers agree that the collaborative relationship between the British colonialists and the Karen of Burma has resulted in a legacy of Burman resentment which has been manifested in the systematic organized violence against the Karen since independence in 1948. In 1947, the new President of the KCO, Saw Ba U Gyi, renamed this national body the Karen National Union (KNU) to more emphatically represent the vision this organization was aiming for – a free and democratic country, Kawthoolei, independent of the new Burma that was being negotiated with a predominately Burman elite group.

The vision for a free and democratic Karen country called Kawthoolei has eluded fulfillment to the current time and now is a faded memory in most Karen's minds and hearts, as they have struggled for their bare survival for more than nearly 70 years. Shortly following the declaration of independence in 1948, the newly formed Tatmadaw (government army) carried out attacks on Karen security posts and villages in Insein outside Rangoon (now Yangon) with large numbers of defenseless Karen killed and their women raped. Their national leader, Saw Ba U Kyi, also a Karen Baptist, and his cabinet, believed they had no choice but to start what became known as the Karen Revolution on 31 January 1949.

The civil war in Burma officially is recorded as taking place between 1949 and 2010 when the step-down of the military junta paved the way for a democratic process to begin. A significant turn against the KNU control of its territory in Eastern Burma during this period began when General Ne Win seized power from the socialist government in 1962 which resulted in a military junta until 2010. When Ne Win came to power, he quickly implemented a very effective "four cuts strategy" to overpower the ethnic armed forces' control in the ethnic areas of Northern and Eastern Burma by cutting revenues, information, recruits and food supply to their various command posts. For the Karen, this was across their seven Brigades in Eastern Burma. The lessening ability of the KNU forces to protect their citizens in the rural eastern Burma areas, resulted in thousands of lives lost, entire villages destroyed, many rebuilt and destroyed again, causing hundreds of thousands to flee everything they thought secure – home, livelihood, religious belief – to become a displaced people in makeshift refugee camps on both sides of the Burma-Thai border from Mae Hong Son in the north to Ratchaburi in the south. These camps were poorly defended, and people were frequently on the move as these displaced Karen sought refuge from the fighting. By 1990, as the fighting showed no sign of reprieve, the UNHCR in consultation with the Royal Thai Government, formed nine official temporary shelters from Ratchaburi in the south to Mae Hong Son in the north which have offered a degree of security, albeit in a foreign land.

While Christianity has never been the majority religion of the Karen of Burma; nevertheless, it is a fact that since the American missionaries first developed a Karen script to use in the formal education system they started, it has been mostly Christian Karen, with the majority belonging to the Baptist denomination, that has held positions of leadership during these conflict years. The 'dawkelu' vision of Dr. T. Thanbyah and his colleagues back in 1881 has been rent asunder with both a religious and geographical divide. The Buddhist majority population has always been a minority in representation in leadership of the national KNU which has been largely responsible for offensive, defensive and maintenance strategies for the Karen affected by the Tatmadaw's very effective campaign to eliminate any opposition to its government's control. Disenchantment in the rank and file Karen army who have always been majority Buddhist, has led to several splits in the KNU, most notable, the formation of the Democratic Karen Buddhist Army (DKBA) in 1994, who in league with the Burmese Tatmadaw, effected the destruction of the KNU Military Headquarters in Ma Ner Plaw in February, 1995 and the largest displacement of Karen since the beginning of the Revolution in 1949.

Once citizens in the country of Burma, the survivors of the brutality against the Karen over seven decades have been relegated to the position of a displaced people, many living outside their native land for up to the third generation. The KNU is now the main representative of the war affected Karen in the National Peace Process since Burma became recognized as a democratic country in 2015, signing the National Ceasefire Agreement (NCA) in the same year. However, numerous violations of the NCA by both Union Government policies and Tatmadaw armed attacks and other abuses has hindered its progression progression to any viable end to the displacement of hundreds of thousands of the Karen and other affected ethnic groups, and in general, a complete mistrust in the ruling powers of Burma to effect any real and sustainable change.

Through all this fighting, human rights violations and displacement, the Christian Baptist Karen suffered another loss – the loss of their mother church connections, their connection with their Karen Baptist Church Area Associations and the wider connection of the Karen Baptist Convention. The escalation of hostilities in Eastern Burma severed this Christian arm of the 'dawkelu', seemingly irreparably. From those impacted directly in the KNU areas, they were cut off from their faith community living in the established built-up areas of the larger cities and towns not directly impacted by the hostilities. Travel to regional and national meetings and trainings was not possible as the Tatmadaw controlled more and more of the Eastern Burma.

For the Christian Baptist Karen in both Burma and Thailand, the concept of mother church is a central tenet of their faith. Mother church is the church where a person is baptized and becomes a communicant member. That person then has a duty to help support that church for their whole life – in prayer, by giving of their tithe (10% of their income), supporting mission and Christian education work and attending special occasions such as annual meetings, annual thanksgiving service and Christmas celebrations.

By the 1980s, many Karen were displaced, not only from their physical homes, but also their mother churches. Others actually moved as a whole church body. Especially in Christian villages that were destroyed, it would be the pastor who would lead them to seek the safety of the border camps. When they arrived in the camps, the pastor would continue shepherding his flock with the church's same name in the place they had moved to. However, for those people, they were still separated from their Karen Baptist Church Area Associations and the Karen Baptist Convention.

It was this conundrum in the early 1980s that led a group of Karen Baptist church pastors who formerly had office positions in their Karen Baptist Church Area Associations, but unable to fulfil their duties as they were now living in temporary makeshift camps on both sides of the Thai- Burma border, to make the decision to start an organization of the same structure from which they were separated. This idea had been discussed and debated many times during the previous decade of displacement years, but many leaders grieved that creating a separate organization to the KBC would further cut them off from their beloved mother church body. However, with no resolution to the hostilities, under the leadership of Rev. Robert Htwe, first the Kawthoolei Karen Baptist Bible School (KKBBS) was officially opened in June 1983 at Htee Ga Gaw Village in Karen State; shortly followed by the inauguration of the Kawthoolei Karen Baptist Churches (KKBC) in January 1984 with its headquarters in Wallei (Gaw Lay in Karen), also right on the border on Burma side. Six church areas were delineated, each corresponding to six of the seven KNU Brigade areas. Two more were added many years later. Soon after opening, the Bible School had to move to Wallei when their village was destroyed, where it remained for another seven years before moving to its current location in Mae La Refugee

Camp in 1990 where it has expanded under the changed name of the Kawthoolei Karen Baptist Bible School and College (KKBBSC) to offer a four year Bachelor of Theology degree in both English and Karen languages as well as the two year Licentiate of Theology in Karen language only.

It is interesting to note that the KKBC has never had a logo. From its beginning, it was not a choice to start an organization separate from the KBC; it was one of necessity. From that time to now, they continue to hope for a democratic Burma where their people can return to their homeland to live in peace, security and freedom; at which point the KKBC can be disbanded as a separate organization and its members once again join with their originating mother organization, the KBC. This desire has to the current time eluded fruition and at the time of publication of this book, the Kawthoolei Karen Baptist Churches serves as an independent Christian Baptist body alongside the Thai Karen Baptist Convention in Thailand and the Karen Baptist Convention in Myanmar, under the wider banner of the Global Karen Baptist Fellowship.

I first met Rev. Dr. Simon in 2004 when I was a volunteer teacher in KKBBSC for five weeks. That five weeks led me to PhD study where I explored Christian Karen Displaced Identity in the face of decades of displacement. Rev. Dr. Simon was central to my study. He granted me permission to live and teach in KKBBSC for three years from 2007 and inspired me to strive for a fuller understanding of his people and their struggle for peace, security and freedom. Among his many writings, one poem "Our Living Testimony" holds special meaning to me, and with his permission, its first lines inspired the title of my doctoral thesis. The poem speaks of meaning in the present and hope for the future and it has become a Christian anthem to the Karen struggle for freedom:

Our Living Testimony

They call us a displaced people, but praise God we are
not misplaced.
They say they see no hope for our future, but praise God;
our future is as bright as the promises of God.

They say they see the life of our people as a misery, but
     praise God, our life is a mystery.
For what they say is what they see, and what they see is
     temporal.
But ours is the eternal.
All because we put ourselves in the hands of the God we
     trust.

(Rev Dr Simon, 2000).

Rev. Dr. Simon shared the story behind this poem with me. He had attended a camp meeting attended by representatives of many of the non-government organizations who provide services in Mae La Camp. He told me he was struck by how all these organizations were portraying the hopelessness of the refugees' situation; a hopelessness that he did not feel and which he knew was not shared by the other Karen community leaders who were present. On returning to his house, Rev Dr Simon's reflection on this experience led him to write this poem.

On a sultry April evening in 2008, I stood with Rev. Dr. Simon in the open Common Room of KKBBSC overlooking the Karen mountains. I was telling him of my plans to leave Thailand for a new job in Northern Ireland now that my fieldwork had finished. His response to me that evening changed my destiny from a secular professional career to a full-time mission of facilitating higher education for Karen refugee youth; his words forever imprinted on my heart and mind,

"Why would you leave this place to write about my people
in a foreign land where my people do not live?"

More than a decade later, I continue to live and work in this mission in Thailand.

Dr. Shirley Worland

Introduction

I am a Karen Christian, and my name is Naw Hsar Ka Nyaw Htoo Simon. I was born in Rangoon, the former capital city of Burma. When I was eight years old, my parents brought me to Kaw Thoo Lei, Karen State along the Thai-Burma border. After living as a free person in the Kaw Thoo Lei for ten months, the Burmese military attacked Gaw Lay (Wallei in Burmese) village in Kaw Thoo Lei. It was at this time that we escaped to Thailand and became refugees. I was a refugee girl for seventeen years in a crowded refugee camp called Maela Refugee Camp. In 2006, the First Mennonite church in Alberta, Canada, and my godparents Mark and Twilla Welch sponsored my sister and myself to come to Canada. I attended Okanagan College in Penticton, BC, Canada and Carey Theological College, University of British Columbia, Vancouver. After graduating the Master of Divinity program, I returned to Maela refugee camp as a Karen Canadian missionary sponsored by the Karen Baptist Churches of Canada.

Just before I went back to Maela in November 2014, I dreamt that my father was talking happily with Ray Vernon, my church friend at First Baptist Penticton who has passed away. I awoke and prayed "Dear God, my dream is telling me my father is going home soon. Please allow me to spend some time with him. In Jesus' name." God answered my prayer. My father spent seven months with us before he finally went home to God.

Since he passed away, I wanted to write his story, but everytime I held a pen, tears dropped until my brain stopped. After our baby (Saw Sausau Simon) was stillborn in August 2018, I began to write my father's story, mostly my memories of him as a person who loved God, loved his Kaw Thoo Lei Karen Baptist Churches, Bible College, and his family. So here is his story, which I name "Papa" meaning father in Karen language.

—— *Papa* ——

Papa was born on 19th July, 1949, the son of Pupu (Grandfather) Myat Maung, who was the son of Peepee (Grandmother) Ah Ma Ya and Pupu Maung Kin. His mother was Peepee Wah Wah, who was the daughter of Peepee Ma Pway and Pupu Aye. Here follows the memory of his birth as it was retold to me.

Someone rushes to see if he can share this good news about the birth of a child.

"His name is Simon."

"Oh, an English name. English names are popular these days."

"I know. I heard many people give their children's name in English, like Wonderful, Volunteer, Sunday, Gear, and July."

"Well, I don't speak English, but my English is improving when I call these names, hahahaha."

"Today is a big day. The day General Aung San is assassinated. Also, the year is important for the Karen Revolution as it is the year our Revolution starts. I hope Simon becomes a good leader someday."

Papa was born in Naung Bo, a village of devoted Karen Christian farmers. The village has two ponds. The one beside Naung Bo church is used for drinking, and the other is in the farm area, for swimming. The village has a primary school and soccer field. Papa had seven siblings; all grew up in Naung Bo and went to the primary school. Papa's twin aunty Pee Thuthu lived inside the village, and his mom lived on the farm with ducks, cattle, vegetables, and gardens.

Naung Bo has two important stories. First, in 1942, the Japanese bombed the village till the place become a big hole, although no one was injured. Second, in the early years of the Karen Revolution (circa 1950), the Burmese military decided to destroy the whole village, but while they were resting on their way at midnight, they saw a group of men on white horses guarding the place. Hence they left.

—— *Four-year-old Peace Activist* ——

When Papa was four years of age, Pupu Myat Maung has cattle, cows, goats, ducks and a farm. Perhaps there are reasons; perhaps there is no reason. People came and took away his cattle, cows and goats. Soon they only had ducks left in the farm. Pupu found it hard to cope. Peepee started to feel neglected, so one day, she left her home. There was no turning back to Naung Bo. She walked; every step was further from her village. Pupu felt so small, but his ego stopped him to chase after her. She continued walking. Papa noticed and rushed to the village edge to see if he can see her. He called, "Moemoe, please come home." His mom turned around and sees him. He ran to her and held her hand, persistently persuading her to return home. She came home. Growing up, Papa was his mother's boy.

—— *The Promise* ——

Papa exceled in school. He always got the highest mark. Peepee called him to her side and said, "Po Kwa (son in Karen language), I named you Simon because you are special". Papa turned to his mom to face her a little, then turned away. "Po Kwa, I want you to study more. There is no school here after primary school." He said nothing. She continued, "I will send you to Sabodaung to my cousin's house. I know you will be fine because you are a hard worker." Papa gave no reply, but he did not like the idea of leaving home. He loved home. Then she said, "I promise to give you a golden necklace when you graduate."

"Golden necklace?"

"Yes, it is very precious."

"Really? Do you have it?"

"Not now, but I will have it when you graduate. I will put a golden necklace on your neck on the day you graduate from school."

Peepee smiled and felt proud of what she just said. She was grinning to herself.

—— *First Fall* ——

When he turns six, his Moemoe wants to eat mangoes. He climbs a mango tree in front of his house and falls. When he falls, he does not breathe. People assume he dies but he starts to breathe again. His Moemoe feeds him turmeric powder until he is completely healed.

—— *Sabodaung* ——

Sabodaung is the village Peepee hopes her son will move to, for further studies. Pupu, on the contrary, wants his son to become a good farmer like him. Farmers in Burma are very poor. The poor couple talk about their son's future. Here follows my imagery of my grandparents' conversations with each other -

> "Htoo Saw Pa (peepee calls pupu), I will let Simon go to Sabodaung to my cousin Paw Wah Say house to study."

> "Htoo Saw Moe, he is a hard worker. He will make a good farmer."

> "But he loves school. He is very good in all his classes. Naung Bo is too small for him."

> "Up to you. What grade is he in now? Who will provide financial support? You know we don't have money."

> "Thra Htoo Kay and my cousin Paw Wah Say. He needs to help look after my nieces and help her with house chores."

Peepee's heart cries inwardly as she sends her son off. He is in Grade Four and will be attending middle school at Sabodaung.

Sabodaung is a village near Bago, not a city, but more urbun than Naung Bo. Papa arrives and meets his three cousins, all girls. His aunt and uncle welcome him as they have no son. The family sleep in a room. He is alone outside.

Soon he goes to school. No friends yet. The first day is very quiet and upon returning home, he too is quiet. The next morning, he covers his head with his tehgu (man's sarong in Karen) and says nothing.

His aunt asks, "Simon, are you well? Time to go to school."

No response

   "Simon, your cousins are ready. Are you ready?"

No response

   "Simon, have you eaten rice? You will be late for school."

Papa then murmurs something inside his shell. "Let me go home and look after my ducks."

   "Simon, your mom wants a good future for you by sending you here."

   "I don't care about school. I will care for my ducks when I go home."

His aunt stops swallowing the elephants. She carries her baby and walks out. That day, Papa stays home alone, under his red tehgu.

— New beginning —

It is five in the morning. Papa gets up and starts the kitchen fire. He boils water and fills the tea jar with water. While he cooks rice, he is talking to his uncle about hunting. His uncle loves talking guy-talk with him. After he cooks rice, he goes to the field to play soccer, comes home and bathes. Then it is time to babysit the girls. He carries his baby cousin on his shoulder and faces the rising sun, puts his book on the floor and glares at it from time to time to rememorize poems. Math and his other homework are already done the night before. He only needs to memorize the Burmese poem which he must recite that day. School is good. Home is fun with the girls. With them, he gets to play with girls' toys like pots and pans and dolls. After school, he quickly comes home and carries water three times. After chores, he has soccer time, next comes dinner and then he buries himself in his books. That is the reason why his uncle always speaks highly of him to his daughters.

"Look," he said – "your Ko Si has all the time to work, study and go to church. He excels in school; he has time to talk, to pray and go to church. He hunts during the weekend. He has time for everything he loves." "Take him as your role model."

Every day is a routine of discipline, including organizing what to wear. He only has two sets of uniforms. He wears one set while the other set is hung out to dry. As the years pass, he got more clothes, passing some on to his brothers who were still carrying muds back in Naung Bo.

— *Going home* —

The first time returning home is full of fun. It is a long trip riding on a cow cart. When Papa arrives in Naung Bo, he goes straight to the pond with his brothers, for a swim. When they come out from the pond, they get to wear the new t-shirts that Papa brought for them. There is a lot of laughter in the pond. Papa loves teasing his younger siblings. He put smelly insects in his palm that let out a bad odor so that inadvertantly the younger brothers inhale it. They laugh. No brother defines it as bullying because Papa's intention is to bring laughter. Again, he brings eggs and said, 'guys, let's eat boil eggs together.' When the brothers smash the eggs, the eggs are empty.

— *Ler Doh* —

At Rev. Ler Gay Paw's house, Ler Doh town, Papa works hard both at school and home. After living there for a few years, he lives with another elderly lady until he finishes High School. She has a daughter who is disabled, she becomes a close friend of Papa's. She, along with all the siblings, love Papa so much. They all call him their beloved Ko Si. Here he encounters an older relative who becomes his inspiration – Pu K'Serdoh. Pu K'Ser was a Karen revolutionary leader who was among the first who signed up with Ba U Kyi when he formed the Karen National Liberation Army (KNLA). Papa calls him Pagyi Naykawba. Pu K'Ser and KNLA soldiers settled not very far from Ler Doh Township. Here, he hears about Karen villagers being attacked by the Burmese troops, their houses being burnt, and their children are forced to become soldiers or porters. Moreover, the Burmese troops rape the Karen girls. Papa is curious about his people's stories. He must hear it from his uncle Pu K'Ser. Monday to Friday he goes to school and on Sunday he is at church, but some Friday nights and Saturday mornings, he disappears. Nobody knows where he goes except his '*besties*'.

— *Best Friends* —

Papa has many besties, and among them are Dickson, Golo Thaw and Eh Ter Mwee. They hang out like Canadian geese, always flying together. They sing together and call each other 'brother'. They are often seen together at church or weddings or thanksgiving services. They form a quartet and go for mission trips as Ler Doh youth. They enjoy each other's company and joke a lot. At Ler Doh, Papa befriends Tee Shwey Toe. Tee Shwey Toe works at Ler Doh office, faithfully serving his people there. There is a strong brotherly bond between the two of them. One common thing that bonds the two hearts together is their love for the Karen people and soccer. Papa becomes very close to Tee Shwey Toe's family. Papa nicknames his eldest son BaNaGu. When Papa arrives to their home, BaNaGu calls to his Moemoe.

"Moemoe, where is a red tehgu you make for Tee Simon?"

"Here. Go and give him."

"My father gets one tehgu and you get one tehgu, same colour. My mom sews both for you two."

"Thanks Banabanagubanagugubanagu."

"Brother, are you up for a soccer tournament this evening?"

"Should I ask BaNaGu's Moe to cook a big rooster?"

"Your guys' custom?"

"Yes, our custom. Hahahahahah."

It is the two guys' custom to eat a big rooster before their soccer tournament. Another hot potato for them is Karen Revolution talk. They both have dreams to help their people. Papa wants to become a Karen army general.

— *An Ambitious Karen General* —

Papa hopes to be trained in Rangoon military school to become a Karen general. In other words, learn Burmese military tactics to fight for the Karen people against Burmese military. He plans to do it. He sets his mind on it. He applies for it. He takes a bus to Rangoon. It does not work out. Finally, his host from Ler Doh asks about him. Here is a conversation I imagine Papa's sponsor asking about him from one of his besties.

"Where will Simon study after high school?"

"MIT"

"Myanmar Institute of Theology?"

"Yes"

"Does he have someone to support him financially?"

"Not that I know."

"I want to help him."

"I will let him know."

"When will you go to Way Ter Gu (Rangoon/Yangon)?"

"This Saturday."

"Have you eaten?"

"What do you cook?"

"Fish paste and vegetables as always. Fried fish. My nephew went fishing last night. River fish. Snakes. Catfish. Come and have a look."

"You don't have to but thank you. Since you already put some rice on a plate, I have no choice but to eat. Hee hee."

"Do you know if Simon has a girlfriend?"

"I think his girlfriend is from here, nearby village. They are very much in love. She is an animist though. Her mother is a very strong animist."

"Simon is a very hard-working boy. Anyone will love him. Now that he goes to MIT, he may have more options."

"You mean more girls."

"Right. Well, the fish is tasty. Thank you."

"Finish already? Leave your plate there. Don't wash your dish. If you do, you cannot come back to my house again. Hey, you eat very little."

"I finished two plates, Peepee."

"Are you sure? My rice looks the same before you eat."

—— *Myanmar Institute of Theology* ——

Although Papa wants to become an army general, God calls him to become His general. He is trained at MIT to serve his people. Throughout his studies at MIT, Papa studies hard, works hard and always rely on God in everything he does. At MIT, he hears his girlfriend in the village is getting married. He talks to his friend about going back to the village to see the truth with his eyes. Like the doubting Thomas; he needs a proof to believe it.

"I am pretty sure it is her."

"But I need to see her and confirm it myself."

"Do you plan to go see her soon?"

"Let's go to her village and ask her this weekend."

They arrive at Papa's girlfriend's house. Someone has already told the family that Papa will be visiting so they are busy cooking chicken curry for him. "It smells so yummy" says Papa's friend who goes with him.

"I heard a rumor your daughter is tying the knot."

"Not a rumor. It is true. I am giving her to a guy next to our village. He will soon come and pick her up …er… tomorrow. Now, the chicken is getting cold. Why don't you guys enjoy the food before you go?"

They sit down and eat on a small round table. While the two friends are biting into yummy chicken thighs, fish paste with fresh vegetables, Papa could not bring himself to finish one bite. He is swallowing his tears. He returns to MIT and time moves on.

Then, Papa has a new girlfriend at MIT. Friends at MIT are gossiping about them, mostly complimenting the educated couple.

"Wow, these two are very compatible."

"I know. Both smart. Both lovely. Both hard working."

"Oh, and both kind of short."

"The whole family from the girl's side knows him and adores him."

"I know they are meant for each other. They will marry soon."

However, after some years, they broke up. Papa is very hurt as he really thinks she is the one. Yet, his love story continues - one day, a group of students talk about a brand-new student at MIT.

"She is from Taungyi."

"I know her dad. Rev. Johnny Htoo. All his daughters are beautiful."

"That is her, moving like a vessel. Shuuushuuu, stop talking. She is coming here."

The lady the friends are talking about is Naw Ta Blut Htoo; she hardly speaks. She brings dry shrimp paste from Taungyi to share it with her friends at MIT. Papa enters the dining room. His eyes meet the very beautiful new student. Papa recognizes her right away and he recalls meeting her once at the Karen Baptist Convention Annual Meeting at Taungyi. At that time, she was holding an elderly lady's hand and Papa remembers how she swept him off his feet. Now, they meet again, even sitting in the same room, MIT dining room. Their friends are teasing him.

"Ko Si, why don't you try shrimp paste from Taungyi? It has come a long way. Here. Try it."

He puts some on his plate and said "Thank you."

"Well, is it good?"

"Good"(not very convincing face).

He disappears in the back to spit the paste out and wonder why they put sugar in shrimp paste. Sugar has ruined the taste. He comes back.

"Why do you have that face when you say it is tasty?"

"Well, I am licking my fingers, see?"

"Hard to believe. You like the paste because the owner of the paste is pretty, right?"

The guys are teasing and laughing, yet Moemoe shows no emotion. Ta Blut also means grace. As her name, she is very graceful. Many guys try to hit on her but fail.

Papa writes to her, a love letter. She ignores it the first time as he is not her type. Her type is tall, handsome, popular among girls, dresses well, classy, and a city boy. Well, Papa is not totally opposite to her ideal man. He is popular, works hard. Girls like him because he is a good sportsman but not very tall and the way he combs his hair shows he is from a village. On Moemoe's list of potential boyfriends, Papa does not fit. Highlighting his 'villageness', she once sees him coming down from MIT guys' dormitory with his hair hanging upwards, wet and uncombed. He must be in a big hurry that he does not care the world. She feels embarrassed for him. Papa does not even know.

Moemoe dresses in full set. If the top is purple, the bottom is also purple, and sandals and hair clips' color will match, like water lilies. When his friends at MIT see her, they name her a gorgeous vessel, because she moves slowly, gracefully, delicately as if she is about to break if she pushes herself just a little harder.

Although their tastes in life are very different, Papa continues to send love letters to Moemoe with little response from her until he writes this letter.

My Dear Htoo,

I want to serve God and serve my people. If you want me to go as far as I can and be prosperous in life, please say 'yes' to me. Saw Simon.

This short letter changes Moemoe's heart. She says yes.

— A Friend at MIT —

Enoch arrives at MIT and finds it is so hard to study. Hard English words and theological terms and other terminologies give him headache. He becomes friends with Papa and asks him to help him with his studies. They becomes good friends and Enoch becomes Papa's soccer fan.

"Bro Si, are you playing this evening? Got time to help me tonight with my paper?"

"Sure, tonight. Will go to play soccer now."

"I will go and watch if I get time. Man, you run so fast. Everyone is rooting for you."

"Hey, Enoch, you walk with God and God will give you Grace."

"Hahahahahaha. Grace is taken, brother Si."

"Well, you never know."

— The Golden Necklace —

A year before he graduated, his mother passed away. They sent him a message saying his mom is in a very critical situation. By the time he arrived home, she had already passed away.

The time arrives for Papa to graduate but his mom is gone, leaving no golden necklace for him. In fact, she leaves nothing. However, he gets his Bachelor of Theology with flying colors. Everyone who knows him congratulate him and says he has done so well. He is the pride of Naung Boe, a small village where the highest education is primary school. He is a big pride for all who have supported him financially throughout his education. Ler Doh Baptist Church youth are very proud of him because he graduates from the highest Theological seminary in Burma. He is the pride of his relatives who think highly of him, especially his village uncle who keeps saying, "I told you so".

Papa feels a big necklace on his neck – a necklace of honor – which pleases everybody's eyes. He is very proud of what he has achieved and prayerfully thanks his mom for the big 'golden necklace' she promised to give him.

—— *Wanted* ——

His sponsor at Ler Doh expects Papa to come back to Ler Doh to become a Principal at Ler Doh Baptist Seminary. Not just Ler Doh, but many churches want him and keep pursuing him until they get a letter from Rev. Dr. Chit Maung.

Dear churches and organizations,

If you want me to live longer and serve God and our people, let Saw Simon work with me at Myanmar Institute of Theology.

In His service,
Rev. Dr. Chit Maung.

—— *Tying the Knot* ——

Moemoe soon graduates. Papa pops the question and writes a letter to Pupu Johnny Htoo.

Dear Tharadoh (Rev) Johnny Htoo

May God bless you and guide you in all your life as you serve Him faithfully. I am in love with your eldest daughter Naw Ta Blut Htoo and ask you to give me her hand for marriage. I hope to come and see you in person someday.

Hoping to hear from you, Tharadoh.

In His service,
Saw Simon.

Pupu is thrilled to hear the good news about his eldest daughter's husband to be. He sounds mature for his age and a very hard working ambitious young leader. He is very keen to see this MIT instructor whom he kind of adores evidenced by his direct letter to him. While he is thinking that, news in the kitchen is different. Peepee Starry and her friend are talking about this potential son-in-law.

"He must be very old."

"You think Dr. Chit Maung's age?"

"Well, maybe same age or a little younger, I am guessing in his early sixties."

"That is too old for Ma Htoo."

"I think she should not marry him if he is too old, aunty."

"Well, we will see. If he is too old, the ex is a better candidate." (Cough)

"You should focus on your health, aunty. I think you look pale."

"I am seeing a doctor this week."

Pupu soon gets to meet Papa and decide on a date. Peepee sees he is not too old. They agree to set the date for April 22, 1980 at Ker Law city during the Karen Baptist Convention Annual Meeting. There will be a triple wedding this time, with each couple contributing seven hundred Burmese kyat for the reception. It is a great blessing for the three couples. It is going to be a grand wedding because KBC conferences are always big when Karen Baptists from all over Burma get together.

Three months before the wedding, Peepee is hospitalized. She is bleeding very badly in the hospital. Pupu Johnny Htoo arrives at the hospital to visit his dying wife.

"Ha. Tharadoh, you are here."

"Yes. I am going home."

Pupu Johnny Htoo, a pastor at Taungyi Karen Baptist Church, disappears from the hospital. He sees his wife bleeding, so he leaves.

"I think I see uncle."

"Yes, he comes and now he goes home."

"Really? Aunty must be happy to see him."

"But he did not stay. Can't blame him. He is quite scared."

"I cannot believe an ordained pastor is afraid of his wife dying."

"Why not? After all, he is also human."

"I know, but when he preaches from the pulpit, he looks so courageous."

"Well, I cannot say, if I were him, I probably do the same thing. Doctors say all her dying friends are gone. She is the only survivor out of the six uterus cancer patients."

"You mean, there are six patients with uterus cancer?"

"Right. She is the only survivor so far."

"I would be really scared if I were uncle too."

"She is literally waiting for her last breath. Doctors say she has three months left."

"Ma Htoo is getting married on the 22 of April."

"I am sure Aunty wants to see her daughter's wedding."

"Well, life is short. We will wait and see if she makes it to the end of the third month. Sometimes Doctors say three months, but they do not even last that long."

"I wonder why she must go through this terrible disease."

"Although uncle does not visit, I hope he prays for her."

"They got some Lahu and Lisu kids from villages coming to live with them. They can all speak Karen and they pray constantly for her."

"I hope a miracle happens."

And yes, a miracle happens. Peepee stops bleeding and leaves the hospital and off to Kerlaw to prepare for the wedding. People who know about her sickness are amazed at her recovery. She looks smart and fast as lightning.

Now, Pupu Myat Maung, my Papa's dad and some relatives arrive Ker Law, a big city with many visitors, especially for the KBC meeting. When he arrives, he asks for his son, Thra Simon. Nobody knows who Thra Simon is. He is so confused. Now that no one knows his son who is getting married, they will go home, like a group of innocent quails. They pack their bags and head to Ker Law train station, hoping to hop on a train to go to Rangoon and back to Naung Bo.

Meanwhile, Peepee Starry hears that her soon to be in-laws are at the train station. She takes a taxi to the train station and approaching them, she asks, "Are you Simon's father?"

No response, so she figures he is the one. She guides them back to the house nearby the wedding venue to stay for the wedding.

—— *Wedding Dress* ——

Moemoe went off to Kanchanaburi to visit her uncle Benny Htoo. The wedding is just a week away, and she hasn't come back yet. Her absence makes so many people nervous – of course, Papa, but also her cousin in Yangon who is stitching her wedding dress. Her cousin guesses her size and sews the dress a week before the wedding hoping it will fit. Finally, Moemoe arrives at Rangoon to look at the dress. Her cousin finishes the dress at two in the morning. The train leaves at six. Moemoe wears the dress and it is a little bigger than her figure, so she needs to figure out something to solve that. She is not going to worry about that. Right now, she must get the train to Ker Law. Off she goes and arrives. It is the morning of the wedding. She leaves the house, looking very simple but charming. Papa sees her from afar, down the aisle. There she is, the beautiful vessel of MIT. Slowly she approaches him with her father. Then she arrives beside him. He looks at her. He has never seen her wear something like that. To end his curiosity – "What is the knot behind your back?" he asks her. Moemoe raises her eyebrows to indicate don't ask. Only Moemoe knows the wedding dress does not fit her, so she ties the back with a red rubber knot to hold it together.

—— *The Wedding Night and Train Ride Home* ——

The newlyweds have booked a hotel in Ker Law. An elderly relative at Taungyi passed away so the rest of the family head to Taungyi right away. No one can give Papa and Moemoe a ride to the hotel. They try to find a person's house to sleep but all the houses are full. Like Joseph and Mary, their "hotel" is a place where people keep charcoal. Exausted, they fall asleep in a dark cold charcoal storage, with a guest sleeping between them – Moemoe's youngest sister. Since she cannot be a flower girl, her sister promises to take her to the hotel with them. She ends up in a charcoal room with her beloved sister and new brother-in-law. In the morning, they get up to prepare themselves to go home.

The newlyweds along with their relatives hop on a train to go home. Halfway through the trip, Moemoe takes a towel and wets it with hot water and cleans Papa's feet with the warm towel. He can't thank her enough for cleaning his feet. It feels fresh. It feels good. He feels loved. He looks at Moemoe with the most appreciative voice, "Thank you for doing this for me, Eh Lay."

—— *Honeymoon* ——

Papa and Moemoe spend their honeymoon in Naung Boe, Papa's birth village. It is a small village where Papa knows everybody including how many trees there are in their farms and which tree is located behind his aunt's house. It is Moemoe's first time there. She is thrilled to meet all of Papa's family, especially his grandmother who is ninety-five and as cool as a cucumber. Sweet lady who eats tamarind soups every single day. Papa's father is friendly but show no affection, unlike her parents who kiss each other and who kiss their children all the time.

Every day, according to tradition, the newlyweds must go to one house after another - to eat. The villagers are often very quiet but once they talk, they keep talking nonstop.

"You know, Ko Si is our cousin."

"He is like my brother although he is my cousin."

"I am his third cousin, and my husband is his uncle."

"Let me introduce myself. I am his uncle's wife's brother's brother-in-law."

"Me too. I am his second cousin's brother-in-law. Kind of related."

Soon the whole village is related.

— *Separation After Honeymoon* —

Before they plan to return to MIT from their honeymoon, news spread that some Burmese military spies had come to MIT to look for Moemoe. It seems that her visit to her uncle in Thailand had raised suspicion with the military junta. Doctor Victor Salone sends message to Papa saying he should come back to Insein without his wife for the safety of her and MIT too. So Papa returns alone.

Meanwhile, Moemoe becomes a "go around evangelist" and travels village to village in the remote areas of southern Shan state in Burma to worship and encourage in the the faith with villagers. She is pregnant and tired but dismisses any concerns about her pregnancy as "a storm in a teacup". The villagers are very happy to see a "go around evangelist". They tell her that other "go around evangelists" bypass their villages at times because they are too remote, and are thrilled that Moemoe visits all the villages. When the news about her visiting her uncle Benny Htoo in Thailand cools down, Papa picks her up and they return to live together in MIT at Insein.

— *First fight* —

Papa's upbringing is defined by these words: farmers, village, close relatives, rural, simple, trees, farms, loving and quiet. Moemoe's upbringing is interpreted by these words: urban, Karen British captain, Karen soldier, brigadier, pastor, power, competitive, city, straightforward, close and loving. Both families are large. Papa has seven siblings, one girl in the middle; Moemoe has seven siblings, one boy in the middle.

One day, Papa's cousin from the village comes to visit him. She is sitting opposite to the house under a tree at the corner of the MIT soccer field. She is tired. You can see from her pale looking face that she has come a long way and perhaps has not eaten. Moemoe goes to see her. She smiles and asks her to come into the house. The cousin says she will wait for Ko Si, her cousin. Moemoe suggests why can't she come in to wait inside the house. She gives no response - Naung Bo's style. Moemoe goes back home to finish her house chores.

By the time Papa finishes teaching at MIT, he comes home. Moemoe tells him his cousin comes to visit him, but she refuses to come inside. As soon as Papa hears that, the battle starts.

"Who will not come in if you kindly invite them?"

"I told her to come in and wait for you inside, but she refuses."

"Where is she now?"

"I don't know."

"If she comes to visit me, she should be here."

"I already told her to come in."

"She is from a village and does not know Rangoon. Compared to Naung Bo, this is huge. She does not know anyone."

"I know."

"If you know, why she is not here?"

"I told you I did tell her to come in. She does not want to come in, insisting to wait for you. Ok. Next time, your relatives from your village come to visit you, I will tie them to a tree, so they cannot run away."

"Stop crying. I understand. I believe you invited her."

Their first fight as a couple ends with that cry.

—— *The Secret Talk in the Middle of the Night* ——

Papa whispers to Moemoe in the middle of the night as if he is going to kiss her.

"Eh Lay, I want to tell you something."

"Tell me, Eh Lay."

"What do you think if I want to go to the jungle to serve there? Will you go with me?"

"Eh Lay, if I know you want to go there from the beginning, I would not have married you. I hate jungle rough life."

The secret conversation stops there.

—— *Three Diamonds* ——

One night, Moemoe has a dream. One of the three couples who married on the same day as them, come to her to give her three diamonds. She tells Moemoe to take good care of the diamonds because "the better you keep, the more valuable they will be."

Then Moemoe gets pregnant with her first child. Just when she is about to give birth, Papa keeps saying he wants to name his first born.

"Let me name her, ok? Have you already asked someone to name her?"

"I haven't asked anyone. You name our first child."

It is February 14, 1981. Moemoe has small contraction around eight in the evening. Papa drives her to Rangoon hospital and leaves her with a lady who takes care of her. He comes home to pick up a few more things. While he comes home, Moemoe tells the nurses she is about to deliver. The nurses get really irritated when patients seem to know more than them.

"You are just a patient. How do you know better than us?"

"I am about to give birth. My baby is about to come out."

"How can you be smarter than us?"

The baby is born. Moemoe is right. The nurses at Rangoon hospital change their irritating statements to compliments.

"Oh, here. Look at our Karen lady here. She gives birth to her first child like a piece of cake. Take this as a good example. See. Brave lady."

The baby comes out, and it is a girl (me). My nose is identical to my father. Papa arrives and names me Naw Hsar Ka Nyaw Htoo. Papa hopes I will be the star of the Karen people.

Another year passes and they bring a new precious baby girl into the world. This time, Pupu Johnny Htoo gives her a name – Naw Thaw Thaw Htoo. She is a brand-new girl who is very energetic, smart, and ready to face the world. She brings joy to the family and everyone around her.

Another year and eight months have passed, they welcome another new baby girl, Naw Paw Paw Htoo. She is so pretty but fragile. Doctors tell Papa and Moemoe that this girl is weak but if she can eat well, she can overcome all her health issues. She is beautiful and adored by everyone.

Moemoe looks sweetly at her three little girls and remembers her friend's dream,

"God has given me three sparkling diamonds to be treasured in my heart forever".

— MIT Guys Dormitory —

Papa and Moemoe now have the three of us but no house. The MIT men's dormitory is our home. Living under the guys dormitory, keeping discipline and respect, and staying organized is not very easy.

"Hi Saya (Teacher/sir), who are these kids?"

"They are my daughters."

"I didn't even know you have children."

"Their names are Nyaw Nyaw, Thaw Thaw, and Paw Paw."

"What kinds of names to name your kids? Cool."

— Peace Activist at MIT —

One day, there is a big conflict at MIT. Students take control of all the keys to the school.

"No one can open the door. Not main door. No door, whatsoever."

"Are you serious?"

"Yes, no teachers can open the doors, not even the Principal or trustees. But if you want to die, you can try."

Soon the news reaches Papa's ear. It was dark and creepy. He begs for the key from the students and opens the door. They threatened to kill anyone who opens the main door, but as soon as Papa opens the door, they take no action.

— Working with MIT's Principals —

Ever since Papa's graduation at MIT, this has been his workplace. He works closely and learns from his Principals Dr. Victor Salone, then Dr. Chit Maung, Thramu Esther Lwin, and Thramu Dr. Eh Wah.

At a forthcoming MIT staff meeting, the possibilities of sending teachers for faculty development was discussed. Papa was appointed, along with another teacher, to go for further studies. This appointment required one to go to the United States of America, and the other to the Phillipines. Papa chooses The Phillipines and leaves to study a Doctorate of Divinity at Asian Baptist Graduate Theological Seminary in Baguio.

—— *Saying goodbye to the girls* ——

Moemoe is happy for Papa when she first hears about his further studies. We are as cool as cucumbers. Papa will go to the Phillipines. Papa will fly in the sky. That is very exciting. We imagine and talk nonstop about Papa's new adventure. Only when Moemoe helps carry the luggage to the car with us by her side, does she really realize Papa is leaving us for at least three years. From joy on Moemoe's face, came a sudden wave of sadness and she starts to cry. Thaw Thaw picks up on Moemoe's distress and joins in the crying in a key that sounds like a fire alarm. Then I follow my sister, with a different sound of crying resembling distance rain drops. Baby Paw Paw clings to Moemoe's chest and starts sobbing with sounds like a kitty meow. Everyone who comes to say goodbye are searching for their tissues.

—— *At Asian Baptist Graduate Theological* —— *Seminary, Baguio, The Phillipines*

Although Papa is awarded a scholarship, it does not cover all his expenses, so he works. He finds a job at ABGTS campus kitchen as a dishwasher. He is enjoying every aspect of his schooling in the Phillipines. His practicum is in a rural area, and he is very loved by the locals there. His teachers and classmates love him and adore him. Again, he is very involved in soccer and active as the students' sport team leader. Besides, he is excelling in all his subjects.

One time, while doing his presentation, one professor comes to listen. The moment Papa sees him, he asks him why he is there. Doctor Albert W. Gammange Jr. explains the blessings of learning from one another. Papa has a great bond with this instructor. Once he finishes all his classes, he is told he can finish his thesis in Burma. He flies home.

By the time Papa comes back from the Phillipines, I am six, Thaw Thaw is four, and Paw Paw just turns three. The second that Papa arrives home, Thaw Thaw runs to him and embraces him. I am taking my time and Paw Paw is so shy to see Papa. She barely recognizes him. It takes her a few minutes to go to him. Papa brings gifts for us as he always does whenever he is away. He hugs and kisses each one of us.

1987 is good. We get to eat chocolate, noodle fries and ice splash at night. We go for walks in the soccer field at night. We play Cinderella at home. We go to visit each other freely at any time.

— *1988* —

1988, April 22 is Moemoe and Papa's seventh wedding anniversary. Only late in the night time do they recall what day it is. Then they ask Papa's youngest brother to go and buy hot tea and some Burmese snacks for them. The food arrives around eleven, and our cheeks are falling apart. Soon, those good old days are gone for the rest of nineteen eighty eight. I come home and tell Moemoe and Papa my teacher says a spy poisoned our water and food, so from then on, no one dares to drink from our primary school. Spies are everywhere, even at MIT. Spies come in and out until the gate must be closed for security. Thaw Thaw and Paw Paw's nursery school compound is also closed. Pee Kayra says the school dance for this year cannot be practiced. Maybe when the situation gets better, we will start practicing nursery school dance again.

Rangoon is now very quiet. Curfew is announced on the street on a loudspeaker. Papa and Moemoe tell us not to worry. After five in the evening, no one can leave their house. Every day, we look down from our balcony to see colorful demonstrations led by "The Lady". Nurses are in white top and red longyi; teachers are in white top and green bottom; police and government workers demonstrate in trains wearing their uniforms. Hundreds of motorcycles surround "The Lady's" white mini car. Every day is so beautiful, and the demonstrations go on in an orderly and peaceful manner – that is – until one bullet is shot. From thenceforth all the peaceful demonstrations end. A young woman who was to be a bride in a few days looking down upon the peaceful demonstration from her balcony was shot. Instantly, she is gone. After this incident, no one can walk around freely. Everyone stays home. Papa and his friends and students guard MIT at night and teach during the day time. There are days when it is not safe to have classes. One evening, there is shooting at Insein prison. "Imprisoned Karen revolutionaries have started the shooting," they said. Now, the Karen in Insein must be very careful. We sit on the stairs in our house and quietly listen to any order. A lady crosses the street after the curfew hours, and the soldiers stop her.

"Hey you, old lady. Stop right there."

"Dear son, I really need to go to the hospital. Please."

"You cannot go. It is 5 pm sharp - nobody can cross the line."

"My husband is very sick in the hospital. He has not eaten anything. We have no children. If we do, our son must be your age, dear son, please let me pass."

"Can't you hear? Are you deaf? Or do you need a bullet?"

"Please son. Who will sleep beside my husband tonight?"

"None of my business. You want to die with my bullet?"

She is sobbing now. There is no mercy. If she crosses, the young soldier will shoot her. If she takes another step, she will not see her husband tomorrow, so she turns around and heads home.

Another man is also crossing towards hospital. He, too, begs for mercy but there is no mercy for him, he is beaten badly by the soldiers. He is moaning in the street. Moemoe tries to close our ears but there is not enough cover to escape all the sounds and voices.

— 8.8.88 —

A soldier gets a bullet in the chest. He is dying. His friends ask Moemoe for a napkin to cover up the wound. Moemoe is so afraid she can hardly move. She is shaken by the begging. Papa is busy guarding the school. He even walks among the demonstrators in Karen traditional dress. Soldiers start shooting, so they run back to MIT. It is exciting. It is tiring. It is scary. It is life and death. Sounds of bullets are everywhere in Insein. Shooting comes from every direction, from the Insein prison, from the front street and from all sides. We can be the next victim anytime. Once a peaceful prosperous Rangoon has become a battle field.

— *Another Secret Talk* —

In the middle of the night, very hot in Rangoon because it is April, Papa whispers into Moemoe's ear again. The secret topic is the same, yet, this time, the difference is that Moemoe starts this conversation.

"Eh Lay, do you still want to go to the jungle?"

"You mean among our Karen people in the Revolution area?"

"Yes, Eh lay, I want to live in the jungle now. I want to run away from Rangoon."

"Why then didn't you want to go earlier?"

"Because I don't like the rough jungle life. You know how much I love cities, Eh lay."

"I know, Eh lay. I will tell you what to take and what to leave."

"Have you already planned the journey?"

Papa

— *April 1989* —

Pupu Johnny has contacted Pu Htun Shein and ask a few questions on how to leave for the jungle. Pu Htun Shein arrives in Rangoon and meets with the group – Pupu Johnny Htoo and some of his children. They leave Taungyi and travel to Rangoon. They do not stay long in fear that they will get caught redhanded, they leave Rangoon for Own Chit Gown the same night. Fortunately, there is a wedding at Own Chit Gown so they tell the villagers and soldiers they are attending the wedding there.

In the meantime, Pupu Johnny and Papa have already talked. The next week, Pu Htun Shein arrives at our house and right away, we vanish into Peh Nweh Gown village and go to Own Chit Gown the same night. Our family of five, Papa and Moemoe, eight-year-old me, six-year-old Thaw Thaw and four-year-old Paw Paw are in a boat at midnight crossing the river to Own Chit Gown. The moon is shining but there is dead silence. No one talks. We are taught to be quiet and being quiet is already under our belts back at MIT guys' dormitory.

The family reunites, eleven of us. It is already dark, but people are very busy cooking. There are four of us children now as my nine year old cousin has joined us. Papa tells us we are going for a picnic.

"Are we going for a picnic? Where?"

"Bangkok."

"Oh, when?"

"Tomorrow, early in the morning."

"The whole family?"

"Yes, very fun. It will be fun."

"Shuuu, stop talking. Time to go to bed. Picnic is early in the morning, so children need to go to bed now."

In the meantime, the elders have things to discuss too. Pu Htun Shein and Papa talk about the next step to take. Pu Htun Shein instructs Papa,

> "We can take you from here to Twa Nay Gown, my brother's house. Then from Twa Nay Gown to Myeh Yeh, you will be on cow carts to Myeh Yeh, then from Myeh Yeh to Nwa Ta, you will get some villagers who help you carry your bags to the next place. I can guarantee that the closer you are to the Revolutionary area, the safer you will be. What about the books you told me earlier?"

> "They are some personal information and letters that I don't want the government to see. For MIT's safely, the safety of my Principal and all our staffs and our relatives who live there and for our safety, destroy them. Wet them with water until you cannot read anything then put them in a garbage. Here is the key to my house. For some textbooks that I can use for teaching in the jungle, please bring them to me."

> "The books may arrive in a few months. I must figure out how to do. But to destroy your informations, I can do that in a few days."

> "You know backwards and forwards about the trip."

> "Yes, we have sent hundreds of University students, mostly Burmese, from Rangoon since many of them got arrested and killed. Some are injured. Some escape before they are arrested. They pass by almost every day. Your group is big, so we need to arrange it a little different."

At Twa Nay Gown, we hide in a villager house. A spy approaches the house where we are staying. News must spread fast, the military sends out spies in every corner. The owner asks us to hide inside his room. He quickly takes all the sandals and chides that no one makes a noise. It is crowded, smelly, sweaty, and hot inside the small room. Eleven people in a small room is not a piece of cake, especially with the four small children inside. The spy arrives.

> "I heard a family group come through this village. See anyone?"

"No, not a soul," lies the villager.

"But I heard the news they cross the river and come through this way. A whole family."

"I don't know. Would you like a cup of tea? Come and have a cup of tea."

"No, I should be on a way to find out where they are heading to."

"Well, then I will not bother. Go ahead."

As soon as the spy disappears, the villager asks us to come out and be prepared to leave for Myeh Yeh. We leave without saying a word.

The voice is quiet but firm, repeating three to four times at 4 am: "Anyone travelling, get in the cow cart now."

"Now, before you take a cow ride, put some dirt on so you will look like villagers here. Here, put Thanaka too. Splash some waste of cows and pigs on your feet and hands to look dirty. The dirtier you look, the less suspicious people will be."

"Here, put some more."

"I smell like poop."

"Don't worry. Just for a few hours."

All the luggage are put in cow carts covered with old clothes and four people sit on top of those old rags. We cover our heads with old towels, so no one really check us. We are mistaken as villagers going to another village.

Burmese soldiers are whistling at the young girls, my aunts, on the carts, mistaking them as teens from a nearby village.

Now, we arrive at the village. Pupu Johnny, 79, needs help as he cannot walk. The two youngest girls need to be carried. Papa carries Thaw and Moemoe carries Paw. My cousin and I are old enough to walk. There are lots of laughter since we start walking.

"Hey, there is only one Burmese among us."

"I know, why is he travelling with us?."

"He has an eye on our side of the village."

"You mean, he has a crush on a Karen girl?"

It is a difficult time in Burma, yet people find a way to laugh at daily things. Everyone talks but only jokes and shallow talk. No one mentions what is happening in Burma now. The walk is more fun when people enjoy it. Our group is now twenty-two people. Eleven family members and eleven villagers who help carry Pupu and the luggage. Soon, we arrive at Htee Ko Nee where the villagers need to go back and from here on, we get new transportation.

At Htee Ko Nee, we have a big fun picnic. Pupu, Papa, Moemoe and our aunts organize a big party where they put numbers on each piece of paper and ask all the villagers to pick a piece of paper with number. The villagers are very thrilled as they get new clothes from picking a number. Everyone laughs so hard when the only Burmese guy gets a flowery yellowish one-set. Then we eat together. Just before they go back, Pupu prays for everyone and Papa and Moemoe distribute an envelope for each villager containing 200 kyat each.

One lady witnesses, "I have never gotten this much money in my life. I am beyond grateful. Thank you for the new top. I will always treasure this memory in my life."

—— *The Journey Continues* ——

From Htee Ko Nee, we travel with elephants and horses and the Karen soldiers that support our move. Pupu and all the adults can breathe more easily now as we are in the Revolutionary area. However, we are not out of the woods yet. At Saw Mu Plaw, while we are walking, news come in that the Burmese soldiers are hunting for us. We are quickly taken to a cave. Like a group of birds, in Htee Nu Ta cave, we are quiet. There Pupu prays,

> God of refuge, you have saved our people from time to time, in the hands of the Japanese during World War II, in the hands of the Burmese military in the early Revolution time. Even now, you will save us from all harms. May you look after us throughout this journey. In Jesus name, we pray, Amen.

After everyone says Amen, news come in again that the military has passed, and it is safe now to continue with the journey.

It is the first time we have seen elephants face to face – three inches apart. Reactions are not the same. My cousin is fascinated. Thaw Thaw is not afraid to ride on one. Paw Paw keeps her distance. I get dizzy by the look, the smell, and the sight of elephants.

> "Ok. Girls. If you want to ride on an elephant, you need to dress and look like a boy," said a mahout.

> "Why not? I will wear my red pant to look like a boy," replied Thaw.

> "Thaw Thaw is a brave one here."

> "Come, Thaw, Moemoe will change you to a little boy."

> "Will you join in, Nyaw Nyaw?"

> "No. Why the young elephant does not like girls?" I asked.

> "He is a teenager."

Thaw Thaw jumps onto the elephant as if she has done it a dozen times.

—— *Per Na Aye Per Ko* ——

Per Na Aye Per Ko is a village where one of Papa's younger brothers lives. He and his wife and two young children have lived there since they got married. His wife's parents are animists, and they do not like the fact that she becomes a Christian, so the couple decides to start a new life in a remote village. Per Na Aye means "waste of a buffalo", and Per Ko means "flat land". There, my uncle sees me write down something so he asks me - "What are you writing, Nyaw Nyaw?"

"The names of the villages that we pass by."

"How many have you got so far?"

"Seven so far."

"Oh, you even write down the details of the journey."

"Yes, like what we did in each village."

"What grade are you in?"

"Two."

"Smart little girl."

"Uncle, why is this place call Per Na Aye Per Ko?"

No reply. Now, everyone is busy cooking for dinner. The food here is fresh. Fish are fished from the river a few hours before dinner. Vegetables are picked a few minutes before dinner – the fast food version in the deep jungle of Karen state.

After a few days at Per Na Aye Per Ko, we move towards the Karen Revolution headquarters, Ma Ner Plaw. Just before we reach the headquarters, we stop at Saw Hta. Unlike the other poor villages we had passed, Saw Hta is a well busy economic zone. Throughout the journey in the jungle, there are days where all we eat is rice and salt. But when we arrive at Saw Hta, we are served chicken in the morning, noodle at noon and sardines with rice in the evening.

—— First Sunday at Saw Hta ——

Papa preaches this Sunday. Third week of April 1989. His testimony that day is fresh and encouraging, inspiring and welcoming,

> When I was young, I dreamt that I was flying. I flew over mountains, sea, valleys, and cities. That dream has never gone away. The dream is a vision that reflects my life testimony. God has called me to serve my people, and I am who I am today because God is leading me throughout. I was born in the year of 1949 when the Karen people began their Revolution. My life reflects the life of the Karen story. My birthday is July 19, the day they assassinated Aung San, a Burmese leader well respected. It is a day of history for both Burmese and Karen sides. I am born to serve my people. Born in a small village, my parents cannot afford to send me to school, but they sent me away to live with my relatives so that I would have an opportunity to study, first at Sabodaung, then Ler Doh, then MIT and ABGTS in The Phillipines. God has helped me fly through all challenges until today, and he will continue to lead me. I trust we are all called to do something for people around us, because we the Karen people are blessed by God.

—— Ma Ner Plaw Means Field of Victory ——

Paw Paw is on an elephant ride with Pupu Johnny. Thaw Thaw is on another elephant with a few other guys. I am walking with Papa and Moemoe and here is an echo of our conversation in the thick jungle of Kaw Thoo Lei.

"Pomugyi (Oldest daughter in Karen), should Papa carry you?"

"Hu Urr" (indicating 'no')

"Eh Lay, this place is very peaceful. Do you find it peaceful?"

"I like the fresh breeze here. Why is nobody here?"

"Let's sit for a few minutes."

The three of us are sitting on a bamboo bench enjoying each other's company.

"I guess the rest of the group have arrived at the Headquarters. How do we follow them?"

"Elephants' poop."

"Hee hee. I know Papa's direction is elephant poops."

"Be careful Pomugyi, there is a scorpion on your seat."

"Where? Are there scorpions in Rangoon? I don't think so. It looks so different. Let me take a look."

"Just be careful. It is poisonous, Pomugyi."

"Let's continue walking," said Moemoe.

"It is six now. Oh, how much I love the breeze here. So refreshing."

"Oh no, Eh Lay. Let's walk faster," said Moemoe.

"Why?"

"Look at the crosses. This is a cemetery. See the soldiers' name on the crosses? Oh some of them are very young. 15, 16 years old."

"If you are afraid, don't look," said Papa.

"Ok. Just walk faster, please."

The three of us feel the tension as we think about the bushy cemetery on the outskirts of Ma Ner Plaw, the Karen Army Headquarters. However, the bamboos sounding like a violin concerta still our fear. We arrive and Pu Bo Mya, the President of the Karen National Union is tickled pink to welcome Pupu Johnny Htoo back to the Revolutionary area. Pupu Johnny Htoo had left the Revolution. According to his verbal account, it was because he was arrested by the Burmese military, but for some people, they say he went back voluntarily with his fellow friends to hold peace talks with the Burmese military. To this day, the truth is in the gray area; however, Pupu Johnny Htoo's love for his people is undeniable. General Bo Mya knows that fact and loves his uncle. Bo Mya trusts his uncle no matter what they say.

"Uncle Johnny Htoo, I am pleased to have you back. We need you to come back and help the Revolution. You will be one of our advisors here."

"I would rather say a prayer for my people. My last wish before I die is to pray benediction for my people. I want to bless my people."

"Then I cannot stop your wish. But you are always welcome, uncle, to come and visit us here. There is another leader who wants to see you – Pagyi Thu Ko Terru."

Pu Terru also loves Pu Johnny Htoo very much. With his big voice he entered the conversation.

"Look who is here, Uncle Johnny Htoo."

"Uncle Johnny, come and share the thanksgiving service with me. Where are you staying?"

"I believe we are settling in Gaw Lay where the Kaw Thoo Lei Baptist Bible School is. Thra Saw Htoo has already spoken to my son-in-law Simon to help with the Bible school there."

"No matter where you live, I will send people to pick you up for my thanksgiving service."

"When are you leaving for Gaw Lay?"

"In a week."

—— *Gaw Lay (Wallei in Burmese)* ——

Early in the morning, Bible school students are singing. They sing Jesus loves me, save me from sins, Jesus heals me, Jesus loves me, save me from sins. Hallelujah....

At eight, they sing "Meet God first in the morning, meet him there to pray. Your heart will then be happy so happy, all through the day."

The songs remind us of MIT students singing "Great is Thy faithfulness, O God, my Father" early in the morning. We have moved from one Theological Seminary to another, just this time we are not in a city, but a jungle.

A few months in Gaw Lay, it is clear that Papa will be the next Principal when Rev. Jerry Lin retires, and Moemoe is already a Principal at Du Ther Tu primary school. Our house becomes very busy. Moemoe teaches only half a day. Papa teaches all day at school.

"Eh Lay, have you eaten?"

"Already."

"How is school today?"

We have a meeting about how to arrange the school schedule to teach more effectively. Because there are more than a hundred students and few teachers and the space is small, we are dividing the students into two groups – kindergarden to grade two will be in class from seven to twelve in the morning, and grade three and four will be in class from one to five in the evening.

"Brilliant. My wife is always brilliant", compliments Papa.

—— *Thaw Thaw and a Bread for Pupu* ——

Our Gaw Lay house is cozy and very well organized. Pupu and Peepee accupy a room. The three single aunts share a room. Another family live in one room. Our family occupy another room.

"Eh Lay, have you seen Po Mu Ser (the middle daughter 'Thaw Thaw')?"

"A few hours ago, she came home from school."

"Where is she now?"

"She must be home. Ask Po Blay and Po Kay - they are home."

"Have you seen Thaw Thaw?"

"Not now. I am cleaning in the kitchen."

"Has anyone seen Thaw Thaw?"

"No."

"I ask her to go and buy me a bread at a nearby store, Po Si (Pupu calls Papa Po Si)."

"She is a brave girl, Papa. I will go and check for her at a bread store."

Many minutes pass. Papa returns from the bread store without his daughter Thaw Thaw.

"Have you found her?"

"No. I didn't see her."

"Come on. Help find my daughter."

An hour passed. Pupu comes in front of the house and everyone is so worrying where Thaw Thaw is. Anxiety clouds our home, and every eyebrow shows no relaxation.

Moemoe indicates, "You know, Gaw Lay is not a very safe place."

"Well, everywhere is not safe."

"I know, but this can be dangerous."

"Don't worry too much, Eh Lay. Your daughter is smart."

"I know she is but …."

Pupu shouts, there is Thaw Thaw. She comes back holding a bread taller than her, carrying it on her shoulder as if it is a bamboo tree. Every eye can now relax. She is home, smiling brightly, saying, "I went to the store and the lady does not have the bread Pupu likes, so I go to Gaw Lay Thai village to buy bread there."

"Pomu Ser (middle daughter), listen. Next time, you don't find things you must return here, and let an adult know. Don't walk alone, ok?"

"Yes, Moemoe."

"My Pomu Ser is so brave, see? I told you she will be fine. Daddy's girl"

— *January 1990* —

January 1990, our first Christmas in the Karen State as a family is now a history. We hear the Burmese military will attack our village. Everyone is ready to run for their lives; war news spreads fast. At school, my cousins and I talk about what we hear from adults.

"The situation is not good."

"What do you mean?"

"The Burmese military will attack Gaw Lay this summer."

It's hot and humid. Everyone is sweating for fear, sweating from the heat and the news. The rumors about the Burmese soldiers attacking us is everywhere, in the market place, at school, and on the street, but home.

"What will you take with you?"

"I don't know. Where are we going?"

"Don't know yet, but we cannot stay in Gaw Lay any longer."

"Fighting can happen anytime."

"Who will fight with whom?"

"Burmese military against the Karen soldiers. I want to fight too. I remember seeing Burmese soldiers pass by when I was in the toilet in Own Chit Gown. Someday, I will fight them."

"But I am afraid of shootings. I hate seeing people bleeding and wailing."

By the end of January, hearsay becomes reality. In the middle of the night, Pupu, Peepee, Papa, Moemoe, and everyone pack to escape the war in Gaw Lay.

"Have you found a car?"

"Yes, Tee Beetaw will take some of us, and Nyaw Nyaw can follow in another car. They said they have space for her in the back."

It is midnight and the sky is dark and ghostly and scary. Everyone is on the move. Thaw Thaw and Paw Paw leave Gaw Lay while sleeping on my parents' arms, and I am sleeping in the back of a car. Two teenagers are in the back of a car and they put me in between the teens. The teens are laughing because I wear a short red skirt that it opens up every time the car moves faster. When we wake up, we are all in Ler Kaw, a Thai village very close to the border. The shootings start. It is very loud. It shakes the ground we are standing on, at Ler Kaw. Soldiers die. Villagers die too.

Pupu urges everyone to sit down, calm down and pray. He keeps saying you cannot do anything by running or swearing at the Burmese military. Calm down and let us pray.

We sit down and listen to his prayers.

In the meantime, charcoal and rice are scarce as people are sleeping in groups. Soon, things disappear from Ler Kaw villagers' farms.

"Bu Kah Moe, my knife is gone. In my farm. I live here fifty years, and I lose nothing in my farm before."

"Refugees are thieves."

"I will not say that. But I am warning everyone not to leave their knives and tools in the farm. They have nothing to eat that's why they take things from people."

"You are too nice, Mu Kaw Pee."

The two villagers separate and go to their separate farms. Shootings become a norm after a few days, but people do not find it normal. It is frightening every day. Every day, injured Karen villagers are brought across to Thai side.

Ler Kaw cannot host anymore refugees so everyone needs to move to Maw Ker. At Maw Ker Thai village, we attend Thai school. Families are packed in a dormitory place. Charcoal disappears every day. There are no police, only gossip.

"My coconut oil disappears."

"Our charcoal disappears too."

"Hi, Nyaw Nyaw's Moe, everyone's here does not own anything, correct? We all share, right? Here is your coconut oil. I was using it last night."

"Oh, if this madness continues, I do not have any more patience. I am going to swear at people."

"Things will get better."

Here comes the beginning of the refugees' story. One day, some Karen men measure things with ropes, so I ask Pupu Johnny what they are doing. I can still picture my reminiscence of becoming a refugee girl.

"Pupu, what are they doing there? Are they measuring?"

"Right, they are measuring the length of houses to be built for refugees. They are dividing lands for refugees."

"Do you mean…we are now refugees? Oh, are we going to stay there?"

"Yes, this place is Maw Ker refugee camp. You and your parents will go somewhere where KKBBS is located. Maybe Maela refugee camp is where you will stay."

"What is KKBBS?"

"Kaw Thoo Lei Karen Baptist Bible School."

"And, your dad is now a Principal of KKBBS."

"How long will we stay here?"

"We don't know. When war stops and peace rules, we will go back to Kaw Thoo Lei."

"Oh, I am praying that we will go back to Kaw Thoo Lei soon."

"Let's go to prayer meeting now. Can you say a prayer tonight?"

"No, please, no. Next time, Pupu."

The men are working like beavers. The next morning, the small houses are built for each family, and soon all the land is occupied. It is the beginning of Mae Ker refugee camp. People move in, and as soon as they do, they invite people for thanksgiving of the new houses, like housewarming, and in Karen tradition, food is gathered from wherever it can be found to share after the service. Every time, there is a thanksgiving service at people's new house, we, the children, go, whether we are invited or not. We go with plastic bag in our hands to bring snacks and soda drink home. Some people are annoyed to see many children, brand new refugees, at all thanksgiving services, but we do not worry much. All we care about is, food!

"Do you bring plastic bag?"

"Yes, in my pocket. Yours? Where?"

"In my hand. I also bring rubber band to bind the plastic bag for Coca Cola."

"Good idea. Got spare ones? Give me one."

"Here."

Aunty Deena's is having a thanksgiving service for her new house in Maw Ker refugee camp. The service is about to start. Everyone gathers and sits down. More and more children come in until the house is packed, both upstairs and downstairs.

At Aunty Deena's house, people are packed so the house breaks apart. People are shouting. The service has not started. People leave, worrying where their kids are.

"I try to protect them from the Burmese military and now, where are they? Will they die now? Hey, do you see my kids?"

"Calm down, no kids die. Thra Simon's middle daughter sits downstairs, and she is not injured."

"I heard some kids get injured."

"Minor injuries. None is serious."

"How about the newborn and her mom?"

"They are okay. Luckily, they sit in a place where none of the uprights fall. No service will be held until they rebuild the house."

"How about the food they prepare?"

"No worries. Completely devoured by the children."

"I wonder about the children now. They are everywhere, especially at thanksgiving services."

"War is bad, making our kids beggars. Do you see them carry plastic bags and rubber bands?"

"Yes, after they eat, they carry the leftover of the food in plastic bags, both snacks and drinks. Can't believe we are now refugees."

— *Maela Refugee Camp* —

Papa is now the Principal of Kaw Thoo Lei Karen Baptist Bible School. He gets the title, yet teachers and students are now scattered everywhere because of war. Soon after Papa moves to Maela, Rev. Robert Kayto, Rev.

Hsar Moo Sheemo, Rev. Shay Tha, Pa Lay and some teachers work with Papa to rebuild the school. In the meantime, Htee Ger Nee church is built, and the school is next to it. Some families have moved in. Next to our house is Tee Nyo Lay's house.

Here, Papa meets Maela refugee camp leader; his name is Pu Law Htee which means drawn in water. His actual name is unknown as people who come to the Revolutionary area often get rid of their real names. He meets this charismatic new friend who seems to know our people's struggle and does not show any weakness. He knows many officers from Thai intelligence and is not afraid of Thai police.

Legally, refugees are not allowed to leave the refugee camp where they have found sanctuary because they are illegal displaced people who carry no Burmese Identity card nor Thai Identity card. Pu Law Htee also carries no ID card, yet he fears no one. When he encounters a Thai police on his way, he uses humour to ease the situation.

"Hi, where are you from?"

"Maela refugee camp."

"Where are you heading to?"

"Maesod city."

"Show me your Thai Identity card."

"We are minors."

Of course, his answer rubs salt in the wound because Pu Law Htee and those travelling with him are in their forties or fifties.

"You know refugees cannot leave the camp. Now, you are being sarcastic to me. You think I am a joke? Come in the office now."

"Ok. We are coming."

They follow to the roadside office. Pu Law Htee is very calm. Still joking here and there. They sit down. He asks to speak to the Thai Intelligence officer (calls him by name). The police officer calls the police in the Maesod office. In a few minutes, they are released. The police now know who he is. Heading to Maesod with no Thai Identity card is a miracle in itself. Sometimes, he brings the whole family with him, his family and our family. The police stop him on the way. The police say you cannot go, so we return to the camp. After a few hours, we go again. When a man with no fear befriends a man of courage, it is a plus. They push and push until they have some rights to freedom of movement for the refugees.

Pu Law Htee, Pu Taw, Rev. Robert Kayto, Rev. Hsar Moo, Rev. Shay Tha, Rev. Golo Per Htoo, Pu Harvy, Pu Saw Bo, Pu K'Baw, Pu Tun Aung and Papa meet up to plan the layout of Maela camp for people to live, and for a cemetery for their final resting place.

"If we live on the mountain, we can escape flood easily."

"Is the flood annual?"

"Yes, it floods every year according to Pu Lah Moo, our leader, who has set his eyes on this place in case our people become refugees."

"If there is flood every year, we should stay in the mountain."

"That means the cemetery will be by the river."

"That will not work as people will drink from the well and clean up from the river. During floods, dead bodies will…."

"That is true. I guess we need to stay by the river and the cemetery will be on the mountains. Can someone give a motion."

"I give a motion."

"I second it."

The meeting is done. The work starts. Maela refugee camp is a temporary shelter, yet while we live here, this is our home.

These pioneers of Maela, all brand new Maela refugees, in a united heart, in the struggle together to serve their people, with the same vision, for the future of their children, with their creative minds, clear determination, humble hearts, with their own hands, start building.

—— *A Carpenter* ——

One day, a beautiful young lady arrives at the Bible school. It is in April. She comes early to get an application form. She wants to attend the Bible school. She meets a guy building a toilet. He is putting the roof on when she arrives.

"Hello, Tee (uncle in Karen). Is this the Bible school?"

No reply from the guy who is building.

"I want to attend the school here. I need a form."

There is no response. He continues to work for a few minutes. He does not rush.

"May I see the Principal?"

Papa gives no response. He goes inside the house, picks up an application form and hands that to her.

"Thank you, Tee".

He is in his forties, she calls him uncle to show some respect. Then she heads back to Maesariang. Only in the rainy season when school starts in June, she realizes that the guy who builds a toilet is the Principal of her school.

— *First Light* —

The first light is a lamp that we need to pump air with our hands to get the light. It sounds like people passing gas. It attracts many insects into our house, but it gives us light to see in the dark. We carry it to the toilet behind our house. We use it when we have family devotion at night. The pump light is used until it fades away. Sometimes candles are used but candles cost too much.

— *The Jungle Maela Refugee Camp Or Beh Klaw (cotton field)* —

Our camp is called Maela Refugee camp because the majority refugees who have moved here are from Maela Karen village. The village is very close to Thailand. Because of war, many flee into Thailand, and they commence to live in a camp. Another name is Beh Klaw which means cotton field. Before refugees resettle here, the whole area is covered in cotton. The Karen Revolution general Lah Moo asked his daughters to plant cotton to occupy the land before Karen people must run for their lives. He knows that sooner or later his people will become refugees, and he needs to prepare a place for them. Once refugees relocated here – the cotton plantation disappears, but the name remains Beh Klaw, a cotton field.

Until 1990, Maela Refugee camp is just jungle and a cotton field that no one lives in. There is a rumor saying this place was occupied temporarily by thieves. They kill and rob and stay overnight here because no one will come by this jungle. According to Pupu Johnny Htoo, this place was his path during World War II and to the time we first arrived, it continued to be his travelling path. When the Karen started their Revolution, this path served them. Pupu also mentions that this path connected Karen villages even before there is a border. When they finally struck a borderline – Moei River in Thai language, Thoo Mweh in Karen language – was agreed upon as the boundary where Burma and Thailand divides, and Maela is now Thailand. Now, this has become our home, a home for many refugees who escape the war in the border areas.

One night, Papa's youngest brother, who shares a room with another student, is playing a guitar. While playing, two snakes seem to appear out of nowhere and start dancing. My uncle wants to stop playing because he sees the big snakes. His friend chides him not to stop. We are on the other side of the room watching our uncle play guitar with two snakes dancing merrily to the music. Our youngest uncle loses his soul as he continues to play. His friend directs the night orchestra. He slowly calms the snakes and asks our uncle to slow down his music. Miraculously, the snakes dance according to the music and gradually leave the scene.

During this early period, monkeys and tigers come down from the mountains to drink from the river. We encounter them frequently at the river, yet the wild animals do not harm us.

—— *First Generator* ——

The first generator is brought by a group of visitors. Papa uses all the gifts with great care. Papa and the school leaders put the gifts during chapel, in front of KKBBS community. Papa writes a thank you note and writes donor details on the blackboard, then takes a picture together with all the gifts they get. They dedicate the generator, and from then on, we say goodbye to our pump lamp. It makes a noise, like a train, from six to nine every night. One day, a Thai authority who lives nearby comes to check on the generator. He comes to see Papa. "Sawadee Krab Ajarn Simon." Papa replies "Hahahahaha Wadee. Come in Wona (a soldier with title)" welcoming enthusiastically with his broken Thai.

The translator then said, "Thra, the Thai authority says refugees cannot use generator. As Thailand do not host refugees legally, we hope you understand our stand on this. Please do not use a generator from now on."

"The generator is a gift from our donors who want us to use it for our students to read and write at night."

"But you cannot use it as refugees."

"If you don't want us to use, come and take it away. While it is sitting here, we will use it because it is very useful for our students."

The Thai authority does not come back to take the generator, nor does he come back to check on the generator. He disappears from us, and the generator is continued to be used for many years. Since then, we continue to hear the sound of the train every night until it is replaced by electricity in the early 2000s by a Korean Mission Dentist team. Papa stands for us, the refugees, the students, and the people of Maela refugee camp.

—— *One of Our Early Visitors* ——

Our early visitors discover us through many channels. They try to find us, and they find us in the jungle. They must walk fifteen minutes from the main road of Tak Song Yang to the area we live, Maela Refugee camp.

A white couple visit us one day. To this day, we do not know how they found us. During this time, rice, fish-paste and vegetables are all we eat every day. Moemoe asks the visitors to sit down. The couple are very polite. They smile a lot too. They bring something inside a bag. We don't have any special food for visitors so Moemoe puts down the thing they bring in a bag for them.

"Help yourself, please."

They politely smile and ignore the offer. Moemoe pushes again to feed them what they bring for dinner. They do not accept the offer by pushing the bag towards Moemoe. Moemoe comes back to the kitchen wondering why the visitors do not eat what they bring.

"Ma Htoo, have you checked what they brought?"

"No, Po Blay (Moemoe's sister Tha Blay). I am assuming it is something they can eat. They want us to eat. I want them to eat because we have nothing else in the kitchen. Po Blay, go and grab the bag. Let's see what it is inside."

Aunty Blay brings the bag, opens it, and they both burst out laughing. It is a raw chicken, no feathers, just a naked chicken. They giggle and laugh, laugh then giggle in the kitchen. Moemoe feels embarrassed. She laughs and starts cooking the chicken.

A Korean group arrives. They talk in Korean; we talk in Karen. No one speaks English, but everyone communicates. They play with us. They carry us around and join in skipping rope or throwing a plastic ball at cans. They help cook in the kitchen. Older ladies help cook Korean food like kimchi and black seaweed. We worship together and give each other gifts before they go home. Here is our routine when they leave to go home. The whole community will walk with them to the main road to say goodbye. They can come and they can leave, but we cannot go out the camp. Our hearts are tied in love and we want the time to stop, but we cannot control; they have to go home. We let them go with tears in our eyes, in theirs too. Their car leaves; we head home thinking will we ever see them again?

—— *First flood in Maela Refugee Camp* ——

At the end of July 1991, it floods. Maela's creek divides our houses from our school. Children in middle school must go to the other side of the river to go to school. At three in the afternoon, we leave school to go home, but no one can cross the river because the small creek is now flooded to a big river. The water is running strong, so the children arrive at the riverbank and wait for adults to come and pick them up. I am ten years old this year. I am looking for someone to pick me up because I cannot cross the river. The river is coffee color and is rushing fast towards the cave, and we cannot cross it. My friends are all waiting too. I think my uncle will pick me up because I know my Papa is a very busy man. Moemoe will not come because she cannot take me across the river. Secretly thinking, Papa may ask any Bible school student who is strong enough to carry me back. While thinking, I scan people carefully across the river and there, I see, Papa, with his red Karen traditional top, waiting to cross the river. I wonder why he must come himself? Finally, Papa wades slowly towards me and carries me across the river. He piggybacks me tightly so the strong water cannot take me away. I, out of shyness, want to get loose, but Papa is not shaken by my insecurity. Papa carries me, safe and secure on his back.

— *The Second Piggyback Ride* —

At Asian Baptist Graduate Theological Seminary, news arrive that Saw Simon is now in Maela Refugee Camp. Papa hadn't finished his Doctor of Divinity thesis when he left MIT in 1989. Through multiple contacts, Asian Baptist Graduate Theological Seminary gets in touch with him. His professors are keen to help him finish his studies. Finally, he receives a message saying one of his professors, Dr. Albert W. Gammange Jr. is coming. Papa tells us about his visitation.

> Dr. Gammange is a very humble man. He is a man of few words but a very wise man. When I do presentation at the seminary in Baguio, he comes and listens to my speeches. I ask him 'why do you come. You don't have to come'. He simply says 'I come because I want to learn from you.'

He is coming, yet there is no confirmation of when he will arrive. Finally, they said Dr. Gammange is in Maesod, and he will get a ride to the camp. Papa is excited to pick his teacher up at the main road. He tells us he is going to bring his professor home, and Dr. Gammange will evaluate his ministry. His supervisor Dr. Victor has passed away. His place of origin has changed too. He is now in a refugee camp, and he cannot continue his thesis as he has left Rangoon. He is now in a new environment and continuing his thesis is academically impossible. However, he is thrilled to see Dr. Gammange again. Dr. Gammange is in his late seventies, so visiting a refugee camp is not very idealistic for him. Besides, the way from the main road to the school is hard to travel. It takes Pupu Johnny half an hour to reach the school every time he visits us from Maw Ker. Now, Dr. Gammange is very tired after a few steps. Papa told him to hop on his back. With uneasy mind, he lets Papa piggyback him back to the school.

At chapel, Papa introduces his students and co-workers to Dr. Gammage and introduces Dr. Gammage to them.

We are in a refugee camp and they call us displaced people, but God is with us. We are very blessed. We have our own organization called Kaw Thoo Lei Karen Baptist Churches. Our churches are in the refugee camps along the border. Our school is under the umbrella of KKBC. Our school is called Kaw Thoo Lei Karen Baptist Bible School. We have eight teachers and forty students since we came back to live in Maela. The school started in a jungle in Tee K'haw with four teachers and six students. The first Principal was Rev. Jerry Lynn. He served as a Principal for seven years. The first convocation is conducted in war time under the trees. Today, we are growing by the grace of God. I was elected the Principal of KKBBS when war broke out at the border. When we resumed the school in June 1990, many new students came to serve God. By God's grace, we cannot leave the camp, but many of our friends abroad find us in the jungle. They come to encourage, inspire, and help us. We are very grateful for all their help. Today, we welcome Dr. Gammange who has come all the way from the United States to see our ministry here.

Dr. Gammange gives a message at chapel then proceeds to sit down one on one with Papa.

"Simon, tell me how I can help you."

"Dr. Gammange, whatever you see is the wonderful works of God. My supervisor passed away before I finished my thesis and before I could move on with another supervisor, I brought my family to the Karen Revolutionary area."

"Simon, what I have witnessed here speaks louder than what you must write in your thesis. I will go back and talk to our Faculty and we will see what we can do for you. Keep up the good work."

"Thank you very much, Dr. Gammange.

— *Unexpected Immense Flood* —

Every resident of Maela refugee camp who thinks the July flood was mammoth were proved wrong one month later, August 18, 1991. On the night of August 17, the heavens open and it pours all night. In the morning, Maela camp is a sea. Bible school students who get up at four in the morning to cook find their big pots and pans floating on the water. Everyone is busy looking for one another. Mother checks if all her children are beside her. In the meantime, Papa's cousin is expecting, and that morning, she gives birth to a baby girl.

"Aunty delivers a baby girl."

"On no, today? How did they get out from their house?"

"In a huge oil tin tank."

"I see Bible school students taking pictures of their pots and pans on the water. They should take pictures of the newborn baby in a big bottle tank too."

"Don't know if they have camera, but the baby's nickname is Naw Htee Doh, which means Miss Flood."

— *Moemoe's family joins us in Maela* —

Pupu and Peepee live in Maw Ker refugee camp and visit Maela from time to time. After a couple of years, Papa and Moemoe invite them to come and live in Maela camp. Shortly after this invitation, they move here. Papa and Moemoe ask us to take piano lessons from Aunty Maylary Htoo, also known as Aunty Darling Girl, the one who slept between my parents in the charcoal room on their wedding night. Since she moved to Maela, she started Peace Music. Peace Music originates in 1992, and it is a group of pianist students who play on Sundays and have annual music competition. Papa supports Peace Music whenever we have competition.

—— *Pupu Rev. Johnny Htoo* ——

Pupu is loved by the pastor of Tee Ger Nee church, Rev. Shay Tha. Pupu is loved by other leaders and co-workers. He is one of the leaders of KKBC. His benediction is full of spirit. He preaches about love, and he loves everyone. As a World War II veteran, he is visited by his British long-lost friend Neville. They talk for hours. Pupu thinks highly of everyone. One day he calls me by his side.

> Nyaw Po, you love writing and you are a smart girl. I am proud of who you have become. You are good at school. I really admire you. However, that does not mean you are the only granddaughter I am proud of. I am proud of the brave, very friendly and outgoing Thaw Thaw and the lovely and shy Paw Paw too. I love and adore all my grandchildren. All of you are unique in your own ways. I remember while I was serving in the British Army, my sister was a nurse. Her medical terminology is so hard for me to understand. Similar to me, she does not understand our military English. Everyone is gifted. Never look down on anyone, Nyaw Po.

"Yes, Pupu."

"Your birthday is coming, right?"

"Yes, tomorrow, Pupu. February 15."

"I will come if I am able. If I cannot come, I will let your Aunty Blay give you something."

Pupu is very creative. I am excited to see what Pupu will give me because on each of his children and grandchildren's birthday, he prepares something unique for the birthday girl or boy. He never disappoints. Sometimes, he kisses Peepee on her birthday according to her age. At Moemoe's forty-second birthday, he asks Papa to kiss Moemoe forty-two times.

On Feb 15, Aunty Blay hands me a gift from Pupu. It is a NIV New Testament, a pink pocket Bible, handy to carry around.

On the last page of the Bible, Pupu has written fourteen countries that he wishes me to go. I turn 14 that year and his birthday wish is for me to serve in 14 countries - United States, Australia, Japan, China, Indonesia, England, Norway, Sweden, Brazil, Malaysia, Russia, Korea, India, and Argentina.

Papa sees the Bible and hears the story. He keeps that story tight in his heart. Whenever visitors come, he would share this story to the visitors as if someone from his family is prophesying, and someone else is going to do some amazing work someday.

Pupu is on his deathbed, very content and loving. He tells Peepee to shave his beard because he says "we, the British soldiers, must look good even in our sick bed." While he can talk, we visit him, he looks at us with very weak eyes but strong voice, "be kind, be good," he lovingly commands.

"Is there a war, Pomu?"

"No, no war" (white lie to prevent him from knowing KNU headquarters is now under the Burmese military control).

"I can hear the shooting" (He is right. Shooting in Karen State can be heard from Maela camp)

"It is farmers hunting for wild animals."

"Oh Pomu, do you think you can lie to a soldier?"

Pupu Johnny Htoo knows the war is escalating in 1995. Democratic Karen Buddhist Army (DKBA) has separated from Karen National Union. Ma Ner Plaw is gone. Kaw Moo Ra is gone. All the Karen headquarters are gone. Soon the refugee camps will be attacked.

Pupu says this about Maela Refugee camp: "Soon there will be war everywhere, but Beh Klaw is blessed."

Finally, on April 25, 1995, he takes his last breath. He is gone, but his legacy stays in his children's hearts. He is loved by his six daughters, six sons-in-law, one son and one daughter-in- law, and all his grandchildren, plus his church members, old friends, new friends, new born, even the grandchildren in his daughters' wombs. Everyone loves him.

— *New KKBBS Students in 1994-1995 Academic Year* —

Ma Ner Plaw, which means the field of victory, is now controlled by the Karen separatist group called Democratic Karen Buddhist Army. This year, there is war everywhere. War breaks out in many Karen villages causing the number of visitors coming to visit to decrease, even students to attend the school. This academic year, five students enroll, four men and one lady. The number is very small, but the team carries on with studies and activities at KKBBS with no turning back.

Every time, visitors come, Papa will ask each class group to stand, each area to stand to represent their place of origin, their churches, and the history background. For example, he asks the students of 94-95 to stand and say "this year, the number of students are very few because of war."

— *The Year 1995-1996 KKBBS Added a Name* —

Pu Taw and Papa and some key leaders of KKBC have talked about introducing a new program to KKBBS. It will be called Bachelor of Theological Studies and the lessons will be taught in English. The name KKBBS is also upgraded to Kaw Thoo Lei Karen Baptist Bible School and College. Students are excited about the new program; however, besides Papa and Pu Taw, there are no regular teachers of the BTS program.

— *Two Friends from Australia* —

Living in Maela is like living in a big zoo where people can come and visit, but we cannot leave as we wish. In 1994, our first friends from Australia come and stay with us in the camp. They are Rev. Alan Marr and Frank

Jackson. They eat like us and try to adapt to the lives of refugees. This was the first of about twenty visits – each time bringing new friends and family with them. Some Australians help us to get a signal to watch television. They help us put up the antenna that looks like fish bone. They turn it around and around so that we can get a good signal. In the evening, I see Alan and Frank are having a serious conversation with Papa. After that, Alan used his contacts to make our situation known to many Baptists throughout the world and more foreigners come to visit. He arranged for two graduates from Oriental Theological Seminary in Nagaland (India) to come as interns each year and teach BTS classes. Through Alan's connection with our Baptist friends around the world, Oriental Theological Seminary is sending their volunteer teachers to teach BTS students. I remember when Papa introduces them to the students, and everyone is excited to see them, our first two Naga teachers from Nagaland. Papa says let us give our new teachers Karen names – Thra Law Eh and Thramu Kee Lah. They eat, cook, worship, talk, and live with us; they stick with us through thick and thin. They run with us during the Democratic Karen Buddhist Army attack in the mid 90s.

Many years later, Frank's satellite dish brought the inernet to the camp for the first time which helped Papa keep in touch with friends around the world through email.

— Cousin Sheeshopo —

Papa has a cousin. His name is Sheeshopo. He is an ex-musician from Burma who is addicted to drugs and alcohol. He attends the Bible College, and he lives with us. Always being sarcastic, he pees in empty bottles and places them beside his bed, which is the office of the school. The school office is outside our family bed. It is smelly and unhealthy for us.

At the end of the school year, Papa organizes a time for thanksgiving and forgiving service where everyone is welcome to pronounce their wrong doing or repent from their mistakes. They go up and confess what they have done and ask for forgiveness. Amongst the confession, more than half of the students have issue with Sheeshopo, the cousin of the Principal.

A girl goes up, "I find that he is a waste because he does not contribute anything to our class". Another lady confesses, "He does not have to do anything. I just don't like to see him." A man goes up, "I try very hard to be his friend but looks like it is impossible."

Papa does not say anything. He continues to host his addicted cousin until he graduates from the school. My uncle Sheeshopo accepts his school diploma like the others, but he does not have a uniform like others. He wears his cousin's (Papa's) Karen top.

Years later, Sheeshopo is sober, marries and has two beautiful sons. He prays for patients at Maela hospital, for Muslim, Buddhist, and Animist patients as he prays for Christians. He draws no line when it comes to befriending others. He is much loved for the deep faith he has in God. He is well respected for the caring he offers to marginalized youngsters. Maela people love him. (At Papa's funeral on August 5, 2015, he comes. He also is dying but looks so keen to celebrate Papa's life. He passed away one week after Papa. On his deathbed, he says "I am going to praise God with my cousin Simon in Heaven." He dies with a smiling face.) I deeply believe my uncle Sheeshopo, who was unconditionally loved by Papa, continues to experience a deep grace and love from Papa in their eternal home.

—— *Muddy Pond* ——

In the 1990s, people suggest the Bible School to create a pond for raising fish, so when the fish are ready to eat, they can just eat from the pond. But that dream is a waste. In June and July when there is flood, the pond becomes a big muddy sea and all the fish disappear. Papa announces at the chapel; the camp hospital asks if the school can clean its pond because it is not healthy to keep it that way. He requests all healthy guys to dump the muddy water outside and let the pond dry. He announces it for two mornings, but no one takes any action. The next day, after school, wearing sport pants and green shirt, Papa jumps in the pond and starts working. Then his students follow him in the pond, one by one. Soon there is laughter and giggling inside and outside the pond. They finish the work in no time because everybody works hard.

— *January 29, 1997* —

January 28 is my cousin's birthday. She turns seven. Almost all the family members go to her house to worship and eat together. It is a quiet night. In fact, every night is quiet now because they say, "Tonight, the situation is not good." Around 9 pm, Pu Saw Bo shows up at our house to tell Papa "The situation is not good." Everyone knows that Democratic Karen Buddhist Army can attack Maela camp any day. Before that day, DKBA attacked Sho Klo refugee camp, Baw Naw refugee camp, Hway Bone refugee camp, Mae Ra Moe refugee camp and other refugee camps on theThai side of the border. Maela camp is next. Bible school students are given guns to guard the camp. Finally, on the morning of January 29, 4.00 am to be exact, our senses were heightened to the sound of repeating 'tak, tak, tak, tak', shortly accompanied by the explosion of mortar shells. The first bullet hits a skin of a banana tree. We hear it from afar, then the bullets get closer and closer. Papa gathers us to pray. While praying Moemoe needs the washroom, then Thaw, then Paw, then me, then Moemoe, then me again and the cycle continues. Then someone commands we leave. Papa stands firmly and says, "I am not going anywhere. I will wait for DKBA soldiers and talk to them. I will tell them we will go back to Burma when peace rules. Do not force us to go back. Buddha teaches peace. We, Christians, love peace. We both love peace so let us talk peacefully." Moemoe and the rest of us leave our house, the school and the market, and we are heading towards the place where we will escape. On our way, we see our childhood friend, Eh Thi Paw. She is in her house.

"Eh Thi, are you going with us?"

"Yes, I am going. But my grandmom has been hit by a mortar shell. Nau Say's grandmother too."

"Oh no. The grandmother who come to watch TV with us every night?" (I start crying).

Eh Thi and her brother are staying with their grandmother. Eh Thi urges her brother to run.

"No, she is not breathing. Let's go."

Eh Thi's brother has been wailing in his home beside his grandmother. Some people on the other side of the road wailed much louder than him.

"No, Peepee, no. Come back to your sense."

"She is gone. Come. We will bury her later."

"You go ahead, I will stay with Peepee here."

We are heading to sleep in another designated area where everybody sleeps on the ground, everyone includes ants, scorpions, caterpillars, insects, and flies. After sleeping on the ground for one night, there is another news saying there are spies among us. DKBA now knows where we have escaped to. They will come and kill us. Other say there is no safety no matter where we go. Some say, we should go to sleep in a cave. Other say, it is safer to sleep in our own houses.

While we are away, Papa stays home with a few men who decide not to run. Papa with Pu Saw Bo and Pu Dee Pa pray every night. Every night, Papa brings three energy drinks with him to share with the other two prayer warriors.

Let us pray for the safety of our people.

Let us pray for mothers and children who escape the war.

Let us pray for DKBA to regain their conscience that this is not right.

Let us pray for world peace.

Let us pray for our KKBBSC Students and KNLA soldiers who are having sleepless nights to protect us.

Let us pray to God to fight for us.

God answers their prayers. DKBA burnt seven houses on the hill, and when the KNLA soldier kills one of them, the rest return home. They threaten to come back the next day and the next day and the next day, but those become rumors. Now, there are many Royal Thai soldiers who come to guard us. Now, as teenagers, we have our opinions on the Thai soldiers."By the look of their faces and the way they carry guns, they look dependable." They come to visit Papa.

"Sawadeekrab (Hi in Thai) Ajarn (Sir in Thai) Simon. We are here to protect you."

"Sawadeekrab Wona (Captain in Thai). If you need anything, please let us know. We are willing to work together."

— *Post January 1997* —

After DKBA attacked Maela, we live with fear everyday. As teenagers in the camp, besides having no freedom, we are now feeling hopeless. The only refuge we have is to pray every night at church. Many of my teenage friends and myself turn to God for refuge.

"Are you heading to church?"

"Yes, you?"

"Me too. Nyawnyi, at church, your dad always speaks positive things that make me feel secure."

I feel the same when Papa speaks.

"He says the Burmese are more afraid; they are afraid they will lose their positions and powers."

"Yeah, I remember that speech. He says the Burmese soldiers and DKBA soldiers are so afraid to come and attack us. They have to use drugs to come here."

"Remember that part when he talks about people praying for us. He mentions many groups, right? Baptist World Alliance, Asian Baptist Federation, his old school in The Phillipines and churches in Australia and around the world."

"Yeah, I remember."

"Hey, I also feel like I am very secure when I hold my Bible like this."

"Cover your ...?"

"Cover my heart. I must cover my heart with my Bible because I feel like my heart will fall down any time soon. Even the slightest noise scares me; reminds me of the shootings."

At church, Papa speaks again.

> God is on the side of the oppressed. He knows we suffer,
> and he is fighting for us. When many people escape, every
> night God is working for us. When Pu Saw Bo, Pu Dee Pa
> and I pray at midnight, we believe God is fighting for us.

After the attack, we stayed in the dark for three full nights. Papa decides to not turn on the generator for three nights, then on the fourth night, the lights are on again and life goes on, each day with less fear as Papa encourages us every single night at prayer meeting.

— *Shooting from the Plane* —

Sunday services start as usual. 7.00 am is Women's service. 9 am is Sunday school. 11.00 am is noon service and 3.00 pm is youth service. This Sunday, around 9.30 am, there is a big shooting from above. This time, it is from a plane. No one leaves the church. Everyone thinks we will die inside the church. Moemoe prays and we repeat after her.

> Dear God, if today is our last day on earth, accept us in your Kingdom.
> We have gone through many difficulties in life, especially one war after

another. If today is our last day, we hope to rest in peace with You. We trust that we will see our beloved ones who have gone before us. In Jesus' name, we pray. Amen.

It is a time for war and conflicts. That shooting comes from a Thai airplane. According to a source in our Maela refugee camp, the Thai authority received the news that the Burmese military was approaching the camp, so they come and scattered them with an airplane and shootings. Every sound makes us want to run, but this time we do not run. We submit our lives to God.

—— *6.00 pm Prayer Devotion* ——

Prayer meeting starts during the time of Rev. Jerry Lynn's leadership in Gaw Lay. In Maela, the tradition of singing "I survive through prayer," is continued, yet the actual prayer meeting at six every night starts from a covenant between a pastor from South Korea and Papa. The two groups of believers have this covenant, every night at six, "we pledge to pray for you, and we hope you pray for us". After the covenant, 6.00 pm prayer meeting is added to the other services we have at church. After a further attack in January 1997, Papa suggests to an elder at a prayer meeting to choose one prayer verse until the verses add up to 31. The 31 verses represent each day in a month. Elders who regularly pray and choose the prayer verses are Pee Insein, Pu Htun Aung, Pu Taw, Pu Dee Pa, Pu Uu Pee, Pu Body, and Papa. Prayer meeting after the attack is more than a gathering. It is like a secure cave in the KNU Brigade 5. It gives strength to survive the next minute. It is a 15 minutes haven for refugee in Maela camp post-DKBA attack. It is the only hope for war survivors who think there is no hope from the world. It is a place where our cause is known and people pray for us; we are not forgotten.

—— *Rumors* ——

"Day Nyaw, I heard something."

"About what?"

"DKBA will attack again. They send more spies to our camp. This time, the spies are Buddhist monks."

"Where do you get the news, Nau?"

"I heard it somewhere."

"I am very afraid."

After hearing the news, I go to Papa to find comfort and to share my fear.

"Papa, DKBA will attack again."

"Where do you get the information?"

"Many people told me. I am so afraid."

"Pomugyi, Naw Nyaw, what is the point of trying to find out if DKBA will attack or not? Listen, they are not coming to attack. They are very afraid now. Don't worry. Also, we are going to get more friends moving here now."

"How will the camp get bigger?"

"Baw Naw, Shoo Klor, Kwee Lay and the other camps will move here, so Maela refugee camp is going to be the biggest camp along the border here. We have the Almighty God with us so don't be afraid."

I feel powerful just by hearing these comforting words from Papa.

— *First Car of KKBBSC* —

"It is too much price for a second hand car."

"Someone must have lied to Rev. Simon. The car is too old, but the price costs an arm and a leg."

"It is from Chaingmai, not even here in Maesod. I hope our leader does not mistreat us."

These are the criticisms Papa gets when he purchases a white truck for the school. He does not give any credit to those critics. He does not show any resentment or feel sorry for himself. He believes in what he is doing, and he continues to move on with the decision. At 7.00 am, everyone gathers beside the white truck to give thanks to God for a 'new car' KKBBSC gets. Papa asks a pastor to pray for dedication of the car then honk the car seven times. Everyone claps and the car is used since.

Because the car is bought after DKBA attack, every time, they shut the car's door, we thought a bomb is dropped. Within a few months, no one dares to joke about that sound; however, only after six months, things get back to normal. People start to talk about how scared they are even when they hear the sound of a car at night.

— Visitors Post DKBA Attack —

Our first visitors after the attack are Rev. Alan Marr and his friends. He is very curious about the attack. He keeps asking what happened, what we did, where were we, and how are we doing now? Here is my answer.

My mom and all the girls here go to sleep somewhere else for a few nights. The first night beyond the main road. The second night we went to sleep at our friend's place beside a cave because they said it is hard for bombs to get in the cave. My dad never leaves our house. He didn't stop us from leaving but he refuses to run. His words make us feel like there is no secure place except in God. We look up to him for encouragement. He is brave. We thank God for giving us someone like him.

Their visit means so much. Shortly after, Baptist World Alliance leaders including Rev. Dr. Denton Lotz, come to visit us. This is one of an exciting moment because they are world leaders. Their visit reminded us of the first world leader to visit us back in 1990, Nobel Peace Prize Laureate,

Archbishop Desmond Tutu. Archbishop Desmond Tutu shouts, "Perker Nay Ba A Blay Law", which means we will get freedom soon. At that time, our hope was so high. We thought we would go 'home' soon. Now after the DKBA attack, BWA leaders are coming to lift our spirits by reassuring we are not forgotten. Rev. Lotz entitled his message "Do not be afraid".

—— *Jokes on Post DKBA Attack* ——

"Hey, do you remember the attack in January?"

"I know. Did you hear the story about the couple carrying a big bag while running? After the shooting, the couple couldn't lift the bag they carried earlier."

"Haha. That's funny."

But I get the best joke. On January 29 early in the morning, two strong men carry their friend to the hospital. When they get in the middle of the road, the shooting starts. While the two guys who were carrying their friend were trying to decide if they should run or continue to walk calmly, the sick man In the cradle jumps out and runs before the two guys. Hahahahahaha.

—— *1998 Doctor of Divinity Honored to Papa* ——

There is a talk on when is a good time to give an honorary degree to Papa. Asian Baptist Graduate Theological Seminary is offering him a Doctor of Divinity Degree. Everyone is excited to hear the news, especially, his students. He makes us proud of being refugees. The degree will be given inside Maela refugee camp, so it is more exciting.

"What an honor for the whole refugee community?"

"I bet. We are over the moon to hear this news."

"Now, the world will see that refugees are not small. We can be seen and heard now."

Soon, the distinguished personalities arrive from the United States and The Philippines. While Papa is preparing to get his degree, the visitors talk to me in a BTS class.

"Let me introduce to you a young lady, Nyaw Nyaw who is Pastor Simon's eldest daughter."

"Hi everyone. Welcome to Maela refugee camp and our school."

"It is hot and sunny today. Well, we bring our suits and ties to wear for the ceremony. Can you please ask your father if we can wear our T'shirts instead of wearing formal?"

"Of course, I can check that out for you."

I run back to my parents' room.

"Papa, the visitors are wondering if they can wear something simple at your convocation."

"Tell them, they can wear something simple. Or give them Karen tops to go with their T'shirts."

I run back to send the message to the visitors.

"Oh, thank you so much. Tell your dad we are very grateful to wear something simple because in some other Asian countries being formal at such ceremony is very important. Thanks for transferring our message."

—— *Fifty-Year-Old Papa* ——

Papa, a lover of soccer, in his forties, is playing soccer with his students still. Maela refugee camp has many soccer tournaments every year – raining season, KSNG, Karen New Year Celebration. The year 1999, Papa is turning fifty. He announces 1999 will be his final year of playing soccer with his students with KKBBSC team. His last game is an exciting one. Our Muslim and Buddhist friends are rooting for KKBBSC. We, at KKBBSC, are cheering very loudly. We shout so loud, we lose our voices after the game. After KKBBSC win, people are talking.

"Wow, Pagyi must be proud. They win, finally."

"Pagyi plays clean and gives his best, as always."

"I can never forget Wahlay Ray's corner ball. That was superb."

"I know. I wish we can tape the game like they do in the World Cup. This game will be in the history of KKBBSC."

— *A Potential Trip to Australia* —

Baptist World Alliance hopes to have Papa in Australia to receive BWA Human Rights Award. Questions are raised for his potential trip to Australia. Does he have a passport? Does he have Thai ID? Does he carry Burmese ID? If he carries no identity, can he go as a refugee and can he get an exit visa from Thai authority? Is it reasonable to ask for a temporary visit? Will Australia give him visa?

After exploring the potentials, Papa gets an answer from those who take care of his travel issue. By now, he has a small Nokia mobile phone to use.

"Hello, is it Pastor Simon from Maela?"

"Yes, Simon speaking."

"Hi, Pastor Simon, can you hear me?"

"Yes, I can hear you."

Let me tell you about your potential trip to receive BWA Human Rights award in Australia. We will be very pleased if you can come and receive the award here in Australia. The Australian government grants a visa and the Thai authority will grant you an exit visa, which is an excellent news. However, the Thai authority suggests if you choose to leave, you will leave permanently. So, you have two options, Pastor Simon, either you come to Australia to receive the award and settle here, or not.

"I am not leaving the camp."

"Oh … we still need to know your name for the Award. May I ask your surname, please?"

"I do not have a surname, sir. Saw Simon is my name."

"We will put Saw Simon on the award pledge then. Thank you for your time, Pastor Simon."

— *2000 Baptist World Alliance Human Rights Award* —

Everyone in Maela camp is excited. Every house in C1A is prepared to accept guests who come for the award ceremony. Early in the morning, people sweep their houses and water their front areas to welcome visitors to our refugee camp. As a family, our houses are very clean and tidy in hosting Baptist World Allaiance Award that will be given to Papa.

In the year 2000, Papa receives the Baptist World Alliance Human Rights Award. His popularity is speaking out among the Karen people. Meanwhile in Bachelor of Theological Studies second year class, we are discussing this hot potato with Rev. Alan Marr.

"Will Rev. Simon get an opportunity to go around the world?"

"Will he get a special privilege to leave the camp?"

"Can he help us get some special Identities so we can have the freedom to travel and move about?"

"This award has made him a hero, so I want to know how popular is he in Australia?"

Rev. Alan Marr calmly replies our curiosity.

> Thanks for your questions. I understand the Baptist community around the world wants to give this award to him to represent the Karen people and their suffering. It is not about Rev. Simon becoming famous. It is a platform for him to speak for the Karen people. This award is saying the Karen Baptist along the border are not forgotten.

Since Papa received the award, many foreigners now introduce him in a very different way. Papa's popularity is moved to another area. First, he was humble, a carpenter, a toilet builder, a cleaner, a driver, a Principal, a Reverend, a pastor, a husband, and a father. Now, he gets human rights award from BWA. Someone has made him more popular, the former President of USA, Jimmy Carter. Five years before, President Carter received the first BWA Human Rights Award. Now the second recipient is a Karen refugee from Maela camp.

— *Selfless Papa* —

March 16, 2000. The celebration in Maela takes place as Papa refuses to go to Australia. After Papa receives US $1000, he has this talk with me.

"Pomugyi, I want to give the thousand dollars back to BWA to pave a way for our youngsters in the future."

"Oh Papa, why do you give it back to BWA? They give you this for you."

"Um… what do you think if I will build new desks and chairs for the coming year for the students here."

"Awesome, Papa."

Papa uses all his award money for the school's desks and chairs. He and others who help him paint the tables green. He announces it at chapel that these are the gifts from BWA Human Rights Award.

—— *Care Villa Maela Refugee Camp* ——

Care Villa is founded by Tee Mawdecai who is Aunty Maylary's husband. The guys at Care Villa are blind. Some also have lost their feet or hands from war, yet they are full of spirit. I go to teach them English sometimes and sometimes just visit. Everytime they need help with transportation to buy their needs at Maesod, Papa helps them.

—— *Generous but Wise in Money Usage* ——

Moemoe wants to make a PEACE ON THE EARTH sign. Papa suggests they do it like before. Draw and put it on old wood. Or she designs KKBBSC and other letters with soda cans too. It does not cost much money. This time, Moemoe calls two students to discuss this matter.

"We will make something more sustainable. Can you guys tell me what we need?"

"Moe, you can buy better wood in Maesod."

"How much is it going to cost?"

"500 baht."

"That much? Well, you continue to work on the letters. I will ask if Pagyi can help with the money."

She comes back and her face shows she does not get what she wants. The two students continue to work on the letters without saying a word. In a few hours, Moemoe starts moving her flowers around and stops talking. Papa comes down from the house because Moemoe disappears for a while. He is humming and looks very peaceful.

"Poe Tu (another cute name Papa calls Moemoe), come and have dinner."

Moemoe ignores his invitation. She continues to work on her flowers.

"You have a green thumb. Look at your beautiful flowers. Poe Tu, it's late. Come and quickly shower, and let us eat together."

Moemoe continues to ignore him. She does not get what she wants, so this is her way of rebelling. Papa does not give up. He does not speak harsh to her but is persistent. He finally approaches the issue.

"Poe Tu, 500 baht is not a small amount of money. Teachers' subsidies are less than 500 baht a month. We can do something else for the school with such an amount of money. But we will see. Come back now."

'We will see' sounds hopeful to Moemoe's ears. She follows Papa up the stairs to their room. The two students watch and smile at each other.

—— *White Gowns and Caps* ——

Moemoe often has conflicts with the rest of the world in Maela refugee camp because she often is very focused on what she thinks is correct, and some think "Moemoe Htoo is too stubborn." At KKBC meeting, leaders discuss the potential caps and gowns for BTS graduates. Many agree that it should be black like an international Bachelor's degree, but Moemoe is keen to make it white, so she makes it happen. At KKBC annual meeting, everyone points a finger at Papa who seems to please his wife in everything. After hours of talk on what color of caps and gowns, Papa stands up and explains, "Each Institute has their own freedom to choose what color they want for their graduates. If we believe Kaw Thoo Lei is pure, we will go with Moemoe Htoo's designs, white color." Some get angry at Papa and Moemoe for winning all the time. People felt defeated but they know how hard Papa works so they give up their opinions. Sometimes they gossip about them. Most of the time, Moemoe and Papa follow their hearts, and quite often, they are hurt.

—— *A Carpenter ... A Cleaner* ——

During the summer, Papa disappears somewhere like - in the toilet - fixing something or in the school kitchen working on a new bench for the students. He loves handiwork. His work is neat and tidy. He knows his standard and pays full attention to his handiwork, and is always careful.

KKBBSC is growing. By the early 2000s, hundreds attend the school. Every morning at chapel, we get the ugly odour coming out from the toilets. Papa announces the work needs to be done but no one seems to start the work. One day, after school, Papa starts working on it.

"Do you see PaGyi working on the toilets?"

"No, he… what?"

"He starts working on the toilets with his short pants. When I first saw it, I did not know how to react. I was surprised."

After he starts working, some students join him in helping.

—— *I Need You* ——

Papa makes anyone around him feel special. Thramu Htoo Leh known as Moe Htoo Leh is one who finished training in Theology but ends up staying home because she lost her three beautiful daughters in their infancy. She and her husband Rev. Goloper Htoo known as Pa Tago decides to stay low key and to serve quietly. Papa never gives up on what he wants. He pleads with her to come to KKBBSC and work with him.

At first, she ignores him but as days go by with his persistent mind, she accepts the offer. Soon, her husband comes and helps at the school as well.

Every year, Singaporean Karen come to visit us. They come and conduct concerts for us. The children of Maela always have big crushes on the Singaporean team. Among the team, Thra Doe Doh is one of the youth whom Papa keeps an eye on. Papa pleads with him to come and help his students with computer skills. Thra Doe Doh says yes and starts teaching summer camp computer classes. Papa then asks if he can help him full time. Thra Doe Doh gives up his wonderful life in Singapore and comes to serve in Maela refugee camp.

Papa also tells Rev. Robert Kayto (Pa Raw) the same thing when he decides to resettle with his family to Australia.

"We need you here. You are a great source for our school. I need you."

Hearing that, Pa Raw does not think twice. He stays in KKBBSC until today. He visits his family in Australia from time to time but calls Maela refugee camp his home.

— *The Opening of BA Program* —

Bachelor of Arts program is another program at KKBBSC. Thaw Thaw and I with our friends attend this program. At first, the volunteer teachers are from Nagaland, but it is not easy to get regular volunteers like the BTS program. Canberra First Baptist Church hear about this and send in two professors, a couple, to teach for a few weeks. The couple arrive, Mark and Twilla Welch. Papa trusts and adores this couple very much. We have prayed for them since we heard they are coming to teach us. In the BA class, I have so many questions so much that the couple realizes I love to study. Thaw Thaw captures the couple's hearts. They love her pure and easygoing personality. Mark and Twilla visit Maela twice. On their second visit in 2004, they ask Papa and Moemoe if they can sponsor Thaw and I to resettle to Canada.

This question of taking their children for further studies is not the first time. Many urge to sponsor my sisters and I for further studies but our parents always reject them.

—— *Sponsoring Two Students to attend Payap University* ——

Prior to meeting with Mark and Twilla, Papa has a serious talk with a potential sponsor about our further studies. After their conversation, Papa says this.

> "Nyaw Nyaw and her friend Cha Quee will go to Chaingmai to study. Payap University. So be prepared. It will take a few months to do some preparations before you go."

> "Oh, this is a very exciting news to hear."

Finally, Papa lets his children go to study now. I am feeling like my dream has finally comes true. In a few months, Papa is on the phone with someone. The next day, the potential sponsors come to visit again. This time, they will help Cha Quee and I get Thai Identity Cards. Just before they make the final arrangement to help get Thai Identity Cards, Papa said this.

> "If my daughters cannot have their own names, I am not going to allow them to go."

> "We are helping your daughters to achieve better things in life. This is for your daughters' future. Please reconsider our sincere hearts to help."

> "My stand is no."

> "I am very ashamed to be a Karen because of you."

Those words are very hurtful, but Papa keeps calm. He takes his stand. Although he is illegal in Thailand, he refuses to do something illegal in Thailand. This is the irony he lived with and leads us to understand. He is a man full of integrity. Nothing can shake him.

—— *A Man with No Identity* ——

While living in Maela refugee camp, Papa lives truly as an illegal displaced person. He carries no passport, nor any identity. When his friends want him to speak for refugees, they arrange his trip but are always sensitive. By sensitive, I mean if he gets caught for travelling without any identity, he will be arrested for leaving a refugee camp. Every chance he leaves for Bangkok or Chaingmai for a conference, he is given a false name to eat, or get in a hotel by using someone's else name.

When encounters occur and someone who has been to Maela refugee camp discover the contradiction behind his identity, they become confused. But if they are aware of refugees' chronicles, they understand. During coffee break -

"Hi, Pastor Simon, oh, am I not correct? You... are you... you are... Pastor Simon from Maela, right? How come you have a different name tag?"

"You are right, I am Simon from Maela. I was given this name tag."

"Ah, I am assuming this is a sensitive issue. I am not going to ask more questions. Now, excuse me."

While standing, mingling with people at the meeting, people who had visited Maela refugee camp, ask him, 'Aren't you Saw Simon?' and 'if so, why doesn't your name tag reads Saw Simon?' When he has a chance to share, he tries his best to speak for refugees, displaced people and their struggle with illegal status. He is 'Simon', 'KKBBSC's Pagyi', 'Pastor Simon' from Maela, 'Ajarn Simon' for his Thai friends, 'Po Si' for his in-laws, 'Saya Si' for his colleagues in MIT, 'Simon' for his besties, 'Eh Lay' for his wife, and 'Papa' for his daughters. Papa never shows resentment when he is mistaken for a different name tag he wears at the conference; however, he is hurt because he is not able to have his own name on his name tag.

—— *Giving Himself Permission to Travel* ——

Being a man with no documents that properly identified and legitimated him placed him in harm's way whenever he traveled and was checked by Thai police. Thai authority does not recognize refugees in Thailand and refuses them legal status. Here is a conversation between two Bible college students.

"Have you ever left Maela?"

"A few times but very scared police will catch us."

"I bet some people carry some identities to travel. PaGyi must have Thai identity or Burmese identity to be able to travel. I see him go to Maesod, Chiangmai, and Bangkok."

"Believe it or not, he does not have Thai ID nor Burmese ID."

"So, what does he carry?"

"He carries his own paper of permission."

"What do you mean? He writes his own letter of permit to leave the camp?"

"Correct. I know. He is awesome. A couple years ago, he was offered the main Thai ID, I mean when you get that, your family can get Thai ID with your surname included, but he chooses not to do it."

"Why did he refuse to have it?"

"Although he gets the main ID, he cannot use his own name, his own age, his own religion, his education and his own village. Knowing PaGyi for years now, he will never do that."

"Some people will see this as a great opportunity."

"Not for PaGyi. He sees things differently. He is selfless in many ways. I think we love him very much because he is the same as us, no public official no identity."

— *Thai Police Verses Illegal Displaced Refugees* —

Whenever Thai police arrest Papa and his students, the police cannot do much with them. He has never been put in jail.

Papa is stopped by police so many times. Whenever they are stopped, Papa will go and talk to the police. He takes the arrest as an opportunity to introduce himself and the refugees. Everytime, the conversations between them follows the same pattern. Travelling with him on many occasions, I can memorize what he tells the police.

We mean no harm to Thailand. We are very grateful to the Thai authority and Thai people for allowing us to live in Thailand. We have many students coming to the camp to learn the Word of God to be equipped for many good works. Thai Karen students come to study with us too. We don't do any illegal things. Please allow us to travel. We will worship there and come back to the camp.

Thai police's point of view and his point of view are contrary.

"You said you are not doing illegal things. This is illegal that you travel with no identities."

"We have a letter with our names on it. Here."

"Who do you think you are? Are you an ambassodor from another country? You wrote your own recommendation letter to travel. Don't forget you are a refugee."

Having his persistent trait in him, he does not give up easily. He continues to explain his case.

We have been refugees since 1990. Since then, we do not commit any crime against Thai law. We help our children to be educated and be prosperous in life. I believe we should have a chance to travel freely because we mean no harm.

It is a contest of who is right and who is wrong. Hearing Papa, the police preaches back at him.

You need permission from your Camp Commander or Provincial leader to travel this far. Who do you think you are that you are able to write your own letter, sign it and travel? Are you an ambassador? Are you making yourself too big? Who are you? I have seen you many times, and your travels make me discomfited.

"But we are travelling to worship and to serve people. Please allow us to go."

The interpreter Teeradet is perturbed to interpret. Teeradet, who is a Thai citizen and lives in Maela as a Karen student, is betwixt and between two cultures. He does not want to interpret for the police because he knows and understands Papa's stand on the point of an illegal displaced person. At the same time, he does not want to interpret for Papa as he knows Thai's laws that illegal immigrants should not travel freely as they wish.

— *Thailand Karen Baptist Convension* —

Annually, when Papa takes his students to Thailand Karen Baptist Convention, they are often stopped by Thai police. The police know many Thai leaders who know who Papa is. Because he is known by some Thai dignitaries in the academic and educational communities, they do not arrest him. Besides the connection he has, Papa is well known by the Karen community in all the camps and much loved, so if they touch him by any means, they are hurting the whole community. The arguments go back and forth until the police' lunch break. One time the police drove out to have lunch, Papa leaves with his students for TKBC annual meeting. Each time, he does not stop going. He is fighting for the rights of refugees' freedom of movement. Observing these things the Camp Commander says this about him: "Where does Dr. Simon get his power from? Who gives him power to do what he is doing?" The answer is God. God is the source of his power.

—— *Finally - Arrested* ——

The Chinese looking police with an impudent black eyebrow stops the car – "Finally, you are arrested," he proclaims.

Papa, Thaw, and Paw get out of the car to talk to the police. Moemoe is alone in the car, waiting as usual. Usually when they visit Maesod, Papa and her girls buy the things she needs; Moemoe waits in the car. Thai police come to her to ask her to leave the car. She looks fretful. Soon the police who arrest them smiles sarcastically and says, "I have been watching you for a while. How come you go around as if you are Thais? You, the father sign here."

"Papa, please wait a little before you sign. P'Nun is on her way to come here."

"What are you waiting for? Sign, here. Here."

"Papa, we know you are not afraid but wait a little."

"Thaw, Papa is not afraid of anything, you know that."

"I know, Pawpi, P'Nun says it is better not to sign."

"Even if we are arrested, they cannot do anything to us, you know that. God will protect us. We have many people who love Papa and support us. No need to be afraid, Thawthi."

"I am not afraid. Just to make things less complicated. If Papa signed, and we are put in jail, things can get more complicated."

Papa listens to his daughters. He waits. Then P'Nun arrives. She talks to the police.

"They have been here for years and have done nothing bad towards Thailand. They educate young people, even Thai Karen youth."

"We are people who follow Thai rules. You are a Thai. You should know they are doing illegal things here. These people are illegal immigrants and they move around like Thai people."

"But they have contributed good things to Thailand. Do you want to talk to my boss? Do you want UNHCR representative to recommend these people? Do you want other Thai leaders to come down here today?"

"I need to arrest them."

"Why?"

"Because they travel illegally."

"No matter what they do, they are illegal. They have been here 15 years and they are still illegal. I know. Because they do not have Thai ID cards, they are illegal. If they buy Thai ID, they are illegals buying people's IDs."

The Chinese looking police disappears and does not show up again. The other policeman who tries to convince Papa to sign is very persistent. He keeps arguing until he gets a call from a police officer above him. He gives up and says "just go." Papa thanks God for the network he has, and many more friends to come.

— *Our New Neighbor* —

One day, a family is looking for a refuge in the camp. They come and live beside our house. The couple has two small children.

"Gaw Ler A Gay (Good morning in Karen), Thramu."

"Gaw Ler A Gay, Dah. I will ask one of my kids to bring pork curry for you."

Bible school students get to eat curry once a month. Every time they have curry, all the teachers receive some as well and sometimes they have extra to share. The generator is on and the students start reading in groups. Moemoe sits down with our new neihgbor.

"I want to bring my youngest sister to live with you."

"That will be great. Is your village very far? When will she arrive?"

"In a week."

As she has said, in a week, her sister arrives, and she starts living with us as our oldest sister, and we call her Nau Mu Mu.

Nau Mu Mu gets up at four in the morning, cooks rice, carries water and picks vegetables. Then she goes to school and comes home and cooks again. At night, she starts cooking vegetables and old rice for the pigs. While the pigs' food is cooking on a pot, Nau Mu Mu shares many stories.

My parents live in KweeJoRo. KweeJoRo is very close to Pa-an. The Karen people in KweeJoRo love each other very much. Buddhist Karen will come and help during Christmas celebration, and Christian Karen will go to help at Buddhist temple during water festival.

"How about your mom and dad?"

"My father is a very quiet farmer. He works very hard every day. Wake up at four in the morning to finish household chores then head to his farm. It will be very nice to have a pair of cows to help him."

"Nau Mu, I want to give him a pair of cows."

Silence.

"I will collect money in my piggy pig to give him a pair of cows."

"Do you have money?"

"Not now. Later. When I become a friend of Thai princess."

We share a laughter.

"Nyaw, you are just like my mom."

"How come?"

"Nyaw is afraid of Ko Per Baw (DKBA), right?"

"Oh, that one is 1000% sure."

I think what my mom is afraid of is not the people but guns. Once a Burmese soldier came to our house, she trembled all over when she poured a cup of tea for the soldier. The soldier asked her, "Ah Moe, are you afraid of me?" She then grasped a bunch of bananas and placed it in front of the soldier, all shaking. Also, the next day, a group of the Karen National Liberation Army arrived too. The soldiers demanded chickens and pigs from the villagers. My mom is afraid of SPDC, KNU, DKBA, anyone who carries guns.

"Really? I always consider the Karen soldier as heros and the Burmese soldier as our enemies."

"Heroes or enemies, they all carry guns."

Time flies when we talk. It is almost 11 pm. Papa calls us: "Po Thay Lee Thay, are you ready for bed? It is getting too late now."

"Ok. Papa. We are done. Coming."

—— *The Reasons More People Come to Live in Maela* ——

This is my neighbor's story. I am including this without putting her real name on it to protect her identity.

My husband and I worked very hard for our Thai landlord who promised to pay us after three months. We ate and fed our kids daily and survived through whatever we had. Then we befriended a few other Karen workers who told us our boss killed his servants before he paid them. They suggested we run for our lives as soon as we can. No one will come to our rescue if we got killed. Our disappearance meant nothing to them. Since we heard the news, we took a line bus and came to Maela refugee camp.

Like our neighbor, my Papa's brother also moved to Maela. Papa's brother who lives in the thick jungle of Brigade Five arrives in Maela with his whole family. His wife looks very pale and white. With his young five children, they arrive, looking really exhausted.

"What is the situation like in P'Na Aye Ber Ko?"

"It is the same. Everyone is farming and commenced hiding their rice whenever they hear the situation is not good."

"Do you mean the Burmese attack the villages."

"Yes, our friends are shot and some disappear without any trace. There are shootings here and there all the time. I think it is time for my children to go to school in a more stable place, so we come."

"Good… you made it alive here."

"Nyaw Nyaw Pa, I cannot see anymore. I wonder if you can help me find a good doctor so I can see again."

"We have Doctor Frank Green and his friends who volunteer at Dr. Cynthia Maung clinic. I will ask them if they come to worship with us here on Sunday. Perhaps they can look and see what they can do for you."

"Will you find us a place to live?"

"I will ask around for a vacant house."

Then the brothers stop talking for many minutes, and the minutes turn into an hour and then they go on with their own business. Papa does his homework, finds his brother a house and arranges his nieces and nephews' who need school.

—— Y2K and Orphanage Dormitories ——

After the 1997 attack, Papa and Moemoe find us more sisters. We become a gang who sing together and hang out together. The house is already crowded in 2000 but Papa and Moemoe decide to open our house to host more orphans and call it another orphanage dormitory. They start by accepting many young children from Htee Moo Ta. We take them to evening prayer meeting and when they come home, the children are already sleeping so we carry them home. Although the name orphanage is used, the children are not all orphans. Many of the kids are children from the Internally Displaced Area.

—— Two Little Brothers ——

One day, an elderly lady comes to see Moemoe. She has something urgent to share with her.

"Can I see Thramu Ta Blut Htoo?"

"Come in, Peepee. She is in the kitchen, cooking and directing, as always."

"Oh, Pee. Let us talk in a quiet place. Here. Sit."

"Thramu, I want to bring two boys to you. Can you raise them? I cannot think of any other place except here."

"Tell me more about them."

I saw them standing beside a road in Maesalit. I was so scared they will meet with human traffickers, so I went and ask them where are they going? The older boy speaks fluent Karen, "we are going to Bangkok to find our mom". The smaller boy is only two. I found out their mom is a girl I know. The older boy's father stays here in the camp but has remarried. The younger boy's dad is unknown.

"Sure. Bring them to us."

At night, Moemoe tells the story to everyone during our family devotion. The next day, the boys arrive. The boys are weak, and both are very beautiful. The younger boy cannot breathe at night due to his asthma. Papa tries to care for him for a little, then Moemoe cares for him for a little, then we take turns caring for him. Thaw May, who is the daughter of Tee Eh Ter'Mwee (Papa's best friend), then takes care of the boys as if they are hers.

— *Teenagers* —

Before the arrival of the small children, Papa and Moemoe's children are cool. There are eight of us. We travel in group. We hang out in group. We laugh together. We fight most of the time. We sing in a group at church. We go to church altogether in group with pretty dresses. We are cool teenagers. We celebrate birthdays, Father's Day, Mother's Day, and Christmas. On Father's Day, we ask money from Papa and buy something Papa needs that year.

"Do you think Papa needs a new belt this year?"

"I think so. His belt is too ancient."

On Mother's Day, we know what we need to buy Moemoe, one set. Top and bottom same pattern and color. We enjoy giving her a new set every year.

On birthdays, we give each other cards full of words in them. Sometimes apologies, sometimes expressing love and sometimes expressing jealousy toward each other. We are all pretty but some are more popular than others so there is teenage rivalry among us.

Our relationship with Papa is kind of unique as we are the closest to him.

First thing Papa does when he gets up is fix his tea. One particular morning he asks, "Po Thay Lee Thay, who prepares a tea pot this morning?"

"It is me."

"You are feeding me chilli, Naw Ter Quee Tha (Banana). So hot."

"Oh, really? Sorry, PaGyi."

Banana thinks she puts dry tea leaves inside the tea pot but ended up pouring chilli inside a tea pot. Some unforgettable memories are saved in our hearts, like Papa reminding us to study. Every night, he tells us to study, study hard. By now, there are three televisions in Maela. Every night, we all come together to watch the television in our house. Thai movies are aired on the television, and the most addicting Thai dramas are aired during final exams.

Although we study, we do it at commercial breaks. During commercials, we run back to our study area to study. It was tricky, fun, and witty to be able to do that.

—— Co-workers of Papa ——

In 2000, Char Quee and I graduate from KKBBSC. We are joining KKBBSC staffs as we finish school. Staff meeting takes place every week at a different teacher's house. This week, it falls in Pa Tago's house. One of our teachers pours out his heart by saying this.

> Each teacher struggles in their own way. I think some families are doing better than others. For example, some families have fewer people. If such a family goes to other another family for thanksgiving, they do not have to cook for that day. If we calculate how many families have thanksgivings in a month and how many times this family goes, we will end up with a big bag of rice that this family does not have to cook for a whole month.

Everyone laughs.

> "My point is I have many children. As each teacher gets 5000 baht a year in KKBBSC, I am finding it hard to host teachers' meeting."

> "We understand, right? We will find a way to solve this."

After that conversation, Papa decides teacher's weekly meeting will take place at the school, and we will eat whatever is served. It will not be a burden to any teacher who struggles financially.

Here Thramu Nee K'Mwee must preach. She speaks about leadership. She talks about leaders with vision. She refers to Papa as a leader who has a vision for his people.

Papa always has a vision for the future of the Karen people. One of his visions is to bring in more leaders of substance, leaders who have integrity. Among many great leaders, he has his eye on Rev. Arthur. As many foreigners visit Maela, Papa often shares the history of the Karen people to them. Many groups arrive. One day, a group of visitors arrive. Papa approaches Rev. Arthur, a pastor from Baw Naw church.

> "Thradoh Arthur, please tell the foreigners about our situation."

> "I think it is better that you do it, Thara Joko (Principal). You have done it so many times."

"I believe you will do a good job. Please take your place."

Rev. Arthur goes up to talk, firmly and slowly to our foreigners.

— *July 19, 2001* —

War is now in the past. Things are looking better now. People are starting to rest from fear. They go on with their daily lives and start to enjoy lives more. Papa's birthday is a big day for KKBBSC. Everyone is excited to give him a special gift every year. They gift him his picture or some new clothes. At Papa's birthday service, all the teachers attend and wish him God's blessings, good health, and a happy, long life. Among the Bible school teachers, Tee C Collar is the funniest one. He is very creative in whatever he does. This year, he is assigned to sing at Papa's birthday. The Chairman calls him up to sing. He goes up with a tape recorder on the stage. People start giggling when they see him with a cassette. He opens the song on his recorder. It is Merdisay's song. It is not karaoke; she is singing. People are more curious now. Then comes the chorus. He joins her by singing tenor for her. Everyone laughs.

— *Family Month Is November* —

Every November, students look forward to hearing their teachers at KKBBSC sing and talk about their distinguished family. Moemoe and Papa is the first couple at KKBBSC. They always sing, "In His Time". They talk about us, Nyaw, Thaw, and Paw. Pa Raw and Moe Raw always sing "Tee Ther Ko A Gay May Yay Shu" (My best friend is Jesus). Pa Lay and Moe Lay sing "Ler Hee Bu, Ta Eh Ta Kwee May Oh" (When love is in our home). Pa Tago and his whole family sing together. Tee Moe sings solo as he has a great voice. Tee Franky always sings with half of his children from a hymnal. Tee C Collar is the creative one. He sings with Karaoke sometimes, alone sometimes, and sometimes with a recorder. Every time, there is a special November family gathering, the program is very enjoyable.

— *9/11 and Maela Refugee Camp* —

Everyone is watching a TV Thai drama attentively when Papa asks for a remote control quietly.

"No, who switched the channel?"

"Important news? … Let us finish the Thai movie then watch the news later."

"Don't say anything, Pomugyi, Naw Nyaw. This is a very crucial news that everyone should know."

"But … Papa …"

"News is important, especially now that World Trade Centre is attacked. Watching real news will educate you to be a good citizen of the world."

But I give my friends a horse face. I want to watch the Thai drama. Papa silences me, and everyone watches the Twin Towers attacked. Papa knows how serious this news is. The room is quiet and serious now. We are watching people jump from the window of the burning building knowing they will die anyway.

In Maela refugee camp, after 9/11, there are tensions between Christians and Muslims. We are afraid of each other. While worshiping at church, someone threw stones on the roof. At the market, some teenagers start wearing pictures of Bin Laden and they also sell the T-shirts. At morning market, the only place where everyone gathers to enjoy trading, women are gossiping.

"Kwa Mu, seeing your smile has eased my fear a little."

"Why? I think we are afraid of you people only."

"We are afraid more. Some teenagers threatened to attack us."

"I don't know. I could not sleep for weeks now."

"Me neither. For years now."

"You are exaggerating. This has started since September 11, a few weeks ago."

"Oh, really? It feels like ages. I think you will not talk to me anymore. Seeing you buy my food makes me happy, but tonight, I am sleeping with fear again."

"I hope this chaos will stop soon. I miss the 1990s when Muslim and Christians were friends."

—— *Increasing Network* ——

Like other incidents, the 9/11 incident shall pass too. Soon, Maela camp is changing. Since 2004, refugees start resettling. Many people from Maela resettle to Australia, Canada, United States, New Zealand, Norway, Sweden, Ireland, Japan and South Korea. Papa's coworkers and students are leaving, one after another. Leaders of the camp are leaving, and finally, Papa's daughters Thaw Thaw and I are leaving for Edmonton, Canada to our further studies and for our future. Decades ago, Papa's parents allowed him go for further studies, so the pattern recycles. Papa and Moemoe finally say yes to Mark and Twilla Welch's request, so Thaw Thaw and I arrived in Edmonton, Canada on the seventh of December 2006.

—— *Nyaw Nyaw and Thaw Thaw Studying in Canada 2006* ——

With the help of Mark and Twilla and First Mennonite church in Edmonton, on December 7, 2006, Thaw Thaw and I arrived Canada. Papa writes in our autograph books.

Dear pomu(daughters),

Your Papa has gone through hardships in the past, and it is now your turn to go and overcome them. Be positive. Be a light. Take care of each other. God bless you. Put God first in everything you do. Proverbs 35, 6.

Papa loves you so much.

Papa calls us beside him, kisses us goodbye and hands us US$50 dollars each.

"Papa, why don't you keep the money for yourself?"

"Just take it."

"I saw a Korean missionary hand you US $100 and you gave us all?"

"Take it. You may need it later and use your money wisely."

— Car Accident —

Papa and Moemoe have developed a love for MehLaMuKee. They build a church that connects with a big cross, designed by Moemoe. Every week, they go back and forth between MaeLaMuKee and Maela refugee camp. They have a meeting with the elders there, talking about how they will make that a mission field. One day, Papa went with two other students to MaeLaMuKee. On their way, the driver loses control of the brake, and the car rolled over a few times and landed on trees instead of a deep valley. Local people come by and see them and wonder why they are not dead. If the trees do not hold them, they will all disappear from this world. Once they get out from the car, Teeradet's feet are injured badly. Papa holds his injured foot and massages it. Soon helpers arrive and help bring them back to the camp.

— *New Car* —

The news is not calm like the incident. News spread that PaGyi Dr. Simon is in car accident, and KKBBSC car is in a bad shape. Once the news spread all over KKBBSC alumni and other old friends of Maela refugee camp, who are now residing in Europe, US, Canada, and Australia, they are checking if Papa is ok.

"We heard about the accident. Is Pa Gyi alright?"

"He has helped me a lot in the camp. Let me know if I can help him in any way."

Soon, Papa gets enough money to buy a new car. It is not his car, but KKBBSC's and uses a Thai person's help make the purchase legal. Now, KKBBSC has two cars that travel together everywhere.

— *Elvis in Town 2008* —

In 2008, KKBBSC celebrates its 25th Silver Anniversary. It is a great celebration. It is grand, full of joy and appreciation of the school and God who provides everything refugees need. The school bought a Karen traditional drum to celebrate this prestigious event. Everyone is so excited and happy. Concerts are everynight of the week long celebration. Feeding the crowds every day, Moemoe arranges it with care, love, and lots of scolding. To get a good picture, she arranges each Pastor and Reverend by height. Tall Reverends to stand in the middle and the shorter ones on the side. When it comes to taking the students' picture, the girls to sit in front, kneeling and the boys stand on the side. She is very creative. Papa is pleased with all her arrangements.

She is arranging and instructing all day. Papa, on the other hand, meets one visitor after another. He is so keen to tell them the story of the school. He loves sharing stories. He does not mind repeating the same story many times.

"PaGyi, the Free Burma Ranger team has arrived."

"Welcome, Free Burma Rangers."

Among, all the gifted singers and musicians, there is a special man, Elvis. He appears and some recognize his look. They are so thrilled the news spread in no time. One group sings after another. Then comes Elvis' time. The ladies are shouting very loudly. They die when Elvis gives them a kiss on the cheek. Everyone laughs. The night is gone. Soon it is quiet. Everyone goes home. By home, they mean Chaing Mai, Bangkok, USA, Karen State, and other refugee camps.

— *2008 Cyclone Nargis Hits Burma* —

In May 2008, Cyclone Nargis hits Burma. Many families lost their loved ones. Thramu Say Htoo cannot find her children. She does not know where are they – perhaps alive somewhere or perhaps gone. A boy who comes to live in Papa's dormitory lost his parents and three siblings on the same day. Many people died on trees, by the river and in the field. Many others survived this deadly cyclone. News spread all over the world. People around the world sympathize with the people of Burma and offer their hands to help. Supports are given but they do not reach the hands of the people. As a result, many people flooded to Maela refugee camp to start a new life. Papa is very involved in helping Nargis victims. The camp leader and other leaders decide to help cyclone victims. Although UNHCR has stopped registering new refugees, they can help the new refugees get ration like rice, fish paste, salt, charcoal, and yellow bean.

Among many newcomers, Dawee and Naw Mu decide to move to Maela as well. They talk with Sheeshopo's wife about moving to Maela.

"Do you want to live near KKBBSC school? The Principal is my husband's cousin."

"That is great. We will want to move there. Cannot afford to live in Burma anymore."

"Let me know when you arrive. We will arrange your place to stay."

They are happy to have a new home and settle in Maela. Da Wee helps Papa in building a worship place at MaeLaMuKee and two prayer houses at Thai Karen villages on the mountain.

Dawee also works outside of the camp. One day, he tells his wife, "I will go to work on construction of the Friendship Bridge (Myanmar-Thailand second Friendship Bridge) and need to be there for a long time. I will earn some money for the kids."

After working on the bridge for a while, Maela Refugee camp calls to check refugee residency. It is mandatory for all refugees. Since the boss refused to give him a lift, he calls Banagu who calls Papa, and Papa picks him up from the building site and takes him to Maela.

— *Rev. Nai Kin Maung* —

Rev. Nai Kin Maung arrives in Maela in 2007 and lives in a small house in B4A with a family of eight. Since a family of eight must share a very small space, he decides to send his niece to a dormitory to go to school. He goes to every dormitory in Maela camp, and no dormitory accepts her. She feels small and discriminated for her Burman ethnicity. She finally decides to quit school. Her uncle, Rev. Naing Kin Maung encourages her not to quit. Finally, he hears about Rev. Dr. Simon and the KKBC dormitory.

"Saya (Sir in Burmese), how are you? Have you eaten?"

"I already ate."

"Saya, do you know PaGyi Saya Simon, the Principal of KKBBSC?"

"I have seen him a few times. He has helped and encouraged many of our Kachin and Lahu pastors who come to live in the camp. Why do you ask?"

"My niece needs a place to live to go to school."

"I got his number. Here it is. 0810397794."

"Thank you so much, Saya."

Rev. Nai Kin Maung rings Papa and comes to see him personally to discuss about his niece. Papa simply says, "yes, she can come and live at the dormitory". He thanks God and thanks Papa. His niece has a home to live.

—— *Travelling to KKBC Meeting* ——

A student graduates from KKBBSC in 2002, he goes back to Ler Wah, Brigade 3 to minister there. During this time, the Burmese military is very active in these areas. Wars break out between KNLA and the Burmese military junta very often. People in this area are often displaced. During wars and displacement, the leaders in the church areas of Kolodraw, Hsarmuper, Maeramoe which are in Brigade 3 and 5 meet together at KKBBSC in Maela three times a year to share their stories. The graduate worker calls Papa to check arrangements for a meeting.

"Hello, PaGyi, we plan to come to the meeting again. Ten of us, PaGyi."

"We will arrange the trip for you. Please contact if you encounter any problem."

Shortly after, another phone call,

"Hi PaGyi, our KKBC leaders who plan to come to the meeting are arrested by Thai police."

As soon as Papa hears the news, he brings Pu Taru to the police station. Papa talks to the police in English, and Pu Taru interprets in Thai. It is a hot Wednesday, but he comes and speaks up for them.

These are our leaders from Maeramoe and Maela Oo refugee camps. They come for a four day meeting, and they will go back to their respective refugee camps as soon as they finish KKBC meeting. Please allow them to go to the meeting.

They shake hands with the police and off they go to Maela Refugee camp.

The next annual meeting, the same graduate worker comes to the meeting with his friend. They walk from Ler Wah village to Maera Moe refugee camp to Mae Tha Waw village. When the two of them arrived Mae Tha Waw, he calls Papa.

"Pagyi, I am here at MaeThaWaw but no more transportation for me."

Silence.

"I need help to get to Maela camp from here."

After silence for a whole minute, Papa says, "Sleep there tonight. I will see if you can come tomorrow." The next day, Papa arrives in the morning with Tee Lee Htoo, picks them up and takes them to Maela camp.

After the meeting, the graduate worker needs help as he has no money to go back to Thaw Leh Hta. Papa's office is a small space upstairs. He walks up to his room and tell him about his situation.

"PaGyi, I need help to go to ThawLehHta."

Silence again.

Papa is playing with his cat. He does not make eye contact. His gray Nokia is sitting on his table. His computer is old and has many lines. Papa is talking to his cat instead of answering him. Time has passed almost half an hour. Then he looks at him.

"When will you go back? Have you got a car?"

"Yes, I have told my friend to get a car for us. As soon as I get support, I will leave."

"How much?"

"4000 baht."

"How about motorboat?"

"600 baht for me."

Silence again.

Papa looks as if he is going to the toilet, then he disappears for a little and reappears with 5000 baht on his hands.

Asking permission from Papa is never easy. He keeps silence for a long time. I remember one student asked permission to go home.

"PaGyi, I need to go back to my village."

Papa does not answer. He neither say yes or no. He is staring at something. He makes no sound. Maybe he is thinking. May be he is discerning. Sometimes it takes an hour to get his answer. After one hour, he gives a reply.

"Ok. You can go."

"No worries. The last line bus is gone."

— *Freedom of Movement for Maela Refugees, 2010* —

New Thai Government gives more freedom of movement to the refugees, who carries no identities. Refugees now travel freely on the main road. More and more people can afford to buy motorcycles. People travel from Zone C to Zone A of the camp with motorcycles on the main road.

Since there is more freedom of movement, some of us can travel more freely. Peace Music Group has traveled to a few places near Maela during this period. Peace Music was started by my youngest aunty who teaches piano. Over time, it enlarged to a full set of music when another violin teacher arrived in Maela. They love volunteering their time for their music students. Many young people in the camp find purpose in playing music that lift many hearts of refugees and other villages nearby. In 2010 and onwards, Papa takes these young people to other places to play and sing in different churches. People are blessed to have them. Many more people started to get to know refugees from Maela camp.

—— *Papa on the News in Australian TV* ——

A record of my Aussie friend seeing Papa on Australian TV. While in Canada, I get a phone call from one of my friends.

"Hello Nyaw Nyaw, how are you?"

"I am fine. How is Australia treating you?"

"So so. Nothing to do except taking English classes."

"Don't you enjoy your classes?"

If I know how to speak English, I should have spoken English years ago. I have no appetite to learn new languages. Besides, my teacher does not know us, the Karen, until they see your father speaking on national television here.

"Did you see my father? On TV?"

"Yes, your dad is speaking, and he talks about Karen people. After his speech is broadcast, my teacher asks if I am Karen. I told her, yes, I am a Karen, not Korean. Then she knows."

"Remind me when did you go there?"

"2004."

"Ah, that was six years ago."

"I know. It has been six years, and no one knows Karen until your father appears on TV. You guys are still very famous."

"No, not famous."

"You are treated as if you are princesses in Maela."

"No way."

"Yes way, you are the princess of Maela. How is Canada treating you?"

"Canada is awesome. I have four jobs and four courses to take. Going to Superstore now."

—— *Lots of Traveling* ——

With the opportunity to travel more, comes more responsibility. Papa and Moemoe go to Maeramoe Bible School Convocation, then Maela Oo Bible School Convocation, then Hill Light Seminary Convocation, then Chaingmai Shilo Bible School Convocation, then Chresto Bible School Convocation in Maesariang, then rest a little until KKBBSC convocation, usually by the end of March. In the summer, Papa gets many calls.

"Thradoh, can we get some of your kids to teach at our summer camp?"

"PaGyi, please send two students to Omkoi this year to teach music and English".

"Thradoh, this year, we need 10 students to teach Karen and English to our youth here".

"PaGyi, we need two pianist teachers this year. Your help will be really appreciated".

"Hi PaGyi, we hope you send us eight students who can sing choir and teach choir".

By the end of the school year, Moemoe and Papa take their young people to different Thai villages to teach. Summer is April to May. By mid-May, students come back to the school and start preparing for the next year.

—— *Phone Call with Nyaw Nyaw and Thaw Thaw* ——

Moemoe and Papa taught children to keep praying for us, so the dormitory children, now more than a hundred, is praying for us every single day.

> "Dear God, please help Nau Nyaw and Nau Thaw in
> Canada. Please keep them safe from all harm and use them
> for your glory. In Jesus' name, we pray, Amen."

Moemoe and Papa call us every day or we call them everyday when we have free time. Despite our busy schedules at school and work, our conversation with Papa and Moemoe plays a very vital role. We are charging our hearts when we talk to them.

"Poe Tu (another nickname Papa calls Moemoe), did our daughters call today?"

"Not yet. They are not getting up yet, I guess."

"Did they call yesterday?"

"Yes, they did."

A phone rings from abroad.

"Speak of the devil. Hello, Pomuser (Thaw), how are you?"

"We are fine. Just got back from work."

"Does Nyaw work at Wendy's still?"

"No, she stops working there. She only works at the college, the church, and Orange Julius."

"She told me about how much pressure she gets at Wendys. Is she well?"

"She is doing well. She even has time to watch Korean movies besides her studies."

"How are you with your Greek restaurant?"

"They really like me. They think of me as their family."

"That is a good thing. We think of all the kids staying here as our own children and there they think of you as their daughters. How are Mark and Twilla?"

"They are fine. Thra gets a new job offer, so they may move to another city soon. I have a new teacher who is teaching me how to drive. I call him Sir Ben. He is the husband of Thramu Laurie Minuk, our counsellor at Okanagan college."

"Are you driving every day? How about Nyaw?"

Yes, I am driving on the main road now. Trying to learn parallel parking. It is hardest. Sir Ben said if I get parallel parking, I will pass the driving test. Nyaw? As you know. Our girly goose. She is afraid to drive. She passes the knowledge test easily. But to drive, she is scared. Her friend from First Baptist Penticton is teaching her how to drive in a cemetery here. Only one day though.

"Heeheee, naw Nyaw Nyi."

"When I know how to drive, I will drive her around. I will call you again tomorrow after work."

Ok. We love you. We trust you. We have hope in you. All the kids here want to see you and learn music and English from you. They want to learn so many things from you. Come home quick.

— *2011 Paw Paw Leaving for Canada* —

In 2011 Paw Paw arrives in Canada. She arrives in Penticton with the help of Our Redeemer Lutheran Church and our god-parents Mark and Twilla's help.

We are very happy she gets here and she is happy too, but within a week, she cries every day, missing Moemoe and Papa and Maela refugee camp.

Slowly, she upgrades to the Grade Twelve standard and then she takes a computer program at Okanagan College. After a semester, she is interested in photography so takes a course online on photography.

Paw fills us many stories about Moemoe and Papa and the hundred children living with them and four hundred Bible school students doing well in Maela camp.

— *Heading to the Franklin Graham Crusade* —

"If going to Maesod is a bad idea, then don't even mention Chaingmai."

"Do you hear a hundred of us are going to Chaingmai to hear Billy Graham's son preaching?

"It will cost a lot."

"I don't know what, but I am going. I already put my name in."

"You have Thai ID?"

"Nope."

Papa arranges the trip with some leaders, both Thai Christians and others who are willing to help. They, together, make the trip happen. They rent vans that will take a hundred KKBBSC students from Maela refugee camp to go to Chaingmai. Finally, they are heading to Chaingmai.

At Chaingmai, a hundred Bible school students sing the Hallelujah Chorus in Karen. Papa speaks on behalf of the refugees. To paraphrase some of his speech -

> I wanted to be a general. But God made me his general. I am right now serving in Maela refugee camp and living among my persecuted people who have no rights to travel. But today, we are grateful for the opportunity to come here. God makes everything beautiful in His time.

His speech is followed by the KKBBSC choir.

On their way back to Maela, they stop at a rest area. At a bus stop, many students go out to take pictures, hang out, or go for a small walk or use the washrooms.

"Today, I witness something amazing."

"What?"

I saw a big waste in the toilet bowl. It smells and the color makes me vomit. I did not use that toilet. I walk out and use the other toilet. When I come out, I saw PaGyi goes in the toilet. I almost stop him, but he already went in. I heard him wash the toilet and used it. After a few minutes, I went in to check it, I saw it was clean. I was amazed. What a leader!

—— *Opportunities to Visit Chiangmai, Voice of Peace* ——

More opportunities come for children to leave the camp. This time, to do a recording with Voice of Peace in Chiangmai.

"Eh Lay, Dr. Viggo wants to take some dorm children to visit Chiangmai. I think we will arrange twenty children to go there."

"If you think it is a good idea, then I hope the kids can visit the city during the summer. They can enjoy Chiangmai during their school holiday."

"Any kid or they have specific kids in mind?"

"Children who can sing."

The next morning, all the children who are going to Chiangmai gather in front of the school to start their journey.

For some of you, this is your first time to go outside Maela refugee camp. For all of you, this is your first time to go to Chiangmai. Look for one another. Help and love one another. Put God first in everything you do. We are praying for you.

After Papa's instructions, Moemoe follows, "When you cross the streets, look out for one another. Walk on the same side of the road."

Papa prays for them, and they head to Chaingmai.

— *Fire April 28, 2012* —

Fire starts from our room, the lowest part of our house and the school, then in half an hour, rooms, classes, chapel, library, and toilets are all on fire.

"Fire, fire, fire. Anyone inside the school?"

"Sisi is having a nap in her room alone."

"No.... wake her up then. Go, wake her up."

"Look at the fire, no one dares to go inside."

"Don't worry about her. I saw her running towards the bridge with a big bag on her head. But the rest... All the school's history, medals, and historic valuables are gone, PaGyi and Moe Htoo's belongings are all gone."

"I know. All gone with the fire."

— *Papa and Moemoe receive the news of the fire in KKBBSC* —

On the day of the fire, Papa and Moemoe had gone to Nupoe refugee camp for a KKBBSC alumni's wedding. On the way from Nupoe refugee camp to Maela refugee camp, they stop at an Esso gas station. They let the students in the car who travel with them know the news.

Moemoe tells this to Papa in front of everyone present there.

"Eh Lay, you are a man, you are a Reverend, you are a Principal, you are a father, you are the secretary of KKBC, you are a husband, so be strong."

She says this, kisses him and leaves for KerNehSu village. She does not want to see the ashes. Papa chooses to come back. He stays. He gathers everyone and prays.

— *Fire 2012 – An Unforgettable Picture from An Eyewitness* —

PaGyi has just returned from the wedding in Nupoe refugee camp. An eyewitness shares the story with me,

"I see him stare at the ashes. Everything is gone. He stares with a tiring look, but not desperate. I feel deeply sorry for him. He talks with a foreigner who comes and visits with his Nokia on his hand. He has nothing left except his bag and what he wears that day and a Nokia phone. God gives him his Nokia to be used during this hard time. He calls many friends on his Nokia. They come and visit. They send in donation. They pray. They do what they can to rebuild the school. It is his Nokia that connects everyone. When I think about PaGyi, I think about a dedicated leader who has a good network who loves everyone. I see hope in him".

— *Fire 2012 – Golden Necklace in the Fire* —

Papa has a golden necklace given by Kaw Thoo Lei Karen Baptist Churches on the 24th, July 1998, the day he received his doctorate. The inscription says "In Recognition of Service for Rev. Dr. Simon". When he was little, his mom promised to give him a golden necklace which never happened as she died before his graduation. Knowing this story, KKBC gave him a literal golden necklace. He never wore it except on the day he received it. On the day of the fire, the golden necklace is gone with the fire.

— *Fire 2012 – KKBC Christian Education Department Savings* —

Moemoe is the Director of Kaw Thoo Lei Karen Baptist Churches Christian Education Department. KKBBSC has two cars. Every time Moemoe takes the dormitory children to go to worship at the other villages, they take the Bible school's cars. Moemoe thinks she will save some money to buy a car for the Christian Education Department. Little by little, year by year, she saves the money in cash and keeps it in a bag in their house. Then comes the fire in April 2012. Along with the school buildings and the house, the money is gone.

— *News of the fire reaches Canada – Nyaw, Thaw, Paw* —

The news arrives in Canada within a few minutes of it starting.

"Hello sis, did you get the news from Maela?"

"What exactly happened?"

"My brother told me to tell you that your house all burns."

"What caused the fire?"

"No one knows yet."

"Oh, I see."

"Our Karen Refugee Committee chairman went down there. I will update you shortly."

The conversation ends there. We tell Our Redeemer Lutheran Church about the fire and the church members are all willing to help. One family gives a thousand Canadian dollars to help with the rebuilding. Meanwhile, at Orange Julius, I tell my co-workers of the fire that happened at Maela refugee camp.

"Good morning honey. Are you girls thinking about fundraising for the fire back home?"

"Nope. We don't think we will do any kind of fundraising."

"That is good because I don't want you girls to get into any trouble. Have you written to Bill Gates? He can help you girls. Why don't you write to his foundation?"

"I will give it a try."

That night I email Bill Gates Foundation. They reply very quickly. It is a 'no.'

— *May 2, 2012 My post on Facebook* —

When the Burmese military has a peace talk with the Karen but sends more troops to the border, I couldn't do anything. I WASH THE DISHES.

When we couldn't make it to my grandma's funeral in South Carolina, what do we do? So helpless. I DO THE DISHES.

When I heard the news of fire that destroyed the Bible College, our house, the dorms, the dining room, the library and all the cats, I couldn't do anything, so I DO THE DISHES.

When my dad sounds so tired on the phone, and I can't help him with anything, I DO THE DISHES.

When my mom is afraid and weary, and I can't be beside her and hug her, I DO THE DISHES.

When I am really hopeless, I DO THE DISHES.

Doing the dishes is a way to relax and pray to God. I am talking to the Almighty who creates the Heavens and the Earth, the Son who redeems us, and the Holy Spirit who always dwells among us while I am doing the dishes.

I surrender all. I DO THE DISHES

— Gossip about Fire 2012 —

After the fire, Papa comes home to see the pride the Kaw Thoo Lei Karen Baptist Bible School and College is gone. In the midst of this hard time, people give him their opinion on the fire.

"Look at PaGyi. I am tearing when I see him."

"He does not blame anyone."

"Right. He gathers everyone and prays. He does not cry. He does not question. He just prays."

"Some people said the school is getting famous but the students have premarital sex in the toilets. That is very dirty. It is no longer holy and clean."

"I heard about corruption too. At Pagyi's birthday last year, pigs and chickens are bought for the ceremony. Before they go on the table, some of them are gone."

"Personally, I think God is punishing them for their sins."

"Well, I would think so, but God is gracious and loving and fire can be an accident."

"I think this fire is the work of the military. The military hates PaGyi because his works are recognized by the whole world."

—— Conversation with Doctor Viggo ——

"Hello, Dr. Simon. Yes, I can hear you."

"Dr. Viggo. There was a fire on April 25, the day the kids went to Voice of Peace."

"Any casualty?"

"No and no one is injured. We need your help."

"I am asking my friends here in Denmark and our Danish Covenant Church regarding how to help with rebuilding. We will see what we can do."

"Thank you so much. Please come to Maela camp. Visit us."

Dr. Viggo packs up and comes down to Maela to see for himself how he is going to help in rebuilding. True to his word, he spreads the need for a new KKBBSC to be built. Money from around the world pours in daily.

— *A new leader raised* —

Many people donate, visit, and pray to help rebuild KKBBSC. Papa entrusts Thra Ler Lay Kler Htoo with the money donated to the school. Through this incident, a new leader who is trustworthy is raised, and the school is rebuilt.

— *Rebuilding 2012 – An Injury* —

Within two months, a new KKBBSC building is dedicated. The building is new, but the spirit that brought it into being back in 1983 carries on.

A teen is working with Papa after the fire. He carries some tools with Papa.

"PaGyi, I can do it alone."

"Let's do it together."

"I hurt my toes. I stepped on something."

"Ok. Stop. Let me check. You are hurting yourself."

Papa gets a first aid kit to care for the teen's foot. He slowly applies spirit on the wound and starts putting some yellow liquid on it and blows the wound slowly. While doing that, he tells the teen, "Only do what you can and do what you can to your best ability."

— *Rebuilding – Teaching by Action* —

Another new student is a hard worker. He is young but also becoming a man. His desire is to come and live in KKBC dormitory. He arrives in KKBBSC compound after the fire. The moment he arrives, he helps with the rebuilding. Working closely with Papa, he is nervous, but does his best. He takes a heavy tool to straighten the iron. Papa watches him closely and stops him.

Instead of pounding the iron to straighten it, Papa holds the iron in both ends, binds it onto a pole and stretches it three times. When he puts it down, the iron is now straight. He does not say anything. The new student copies what Papa shows him.

—— *Rebuilding – Mistaken As Another Worker Again* ——

"Hi, Patee (uncle), are you a worker here? I have seen you working almost every day."

Everyone is quiet. No one utters a word. As there is no reply, he turns around and heads back to carry sand from the river.

"Hey, you are funny."

"Why?"

"You talked to the Principal as if he is your buddy."

"Where? Who is the Principal?"

"The one you call Patee."

"Ah, is that PaGyi Dr. Simon? I did not know that. Oh, no. I am very embarrassed."

"No worries. PaGyi is cool. We love him."

—— *A Visit home to a new home and* —— *KKBBSC, July and August 2012*

My sisters and I arrive in Bangkok to visit our parents and Maela. Two months have passed since the fire. In the new dormitory, the kids are talking about us.

"I am not lying. Nau Nyaw, Nau Thaw, Nau Paw were here last night."

"Where are they now? You lie."

"I don't lie. You were in the sack when they got here. They are now heading to Chaingmai with Moemoe and Papa."

"If you lie, give me five baht."

Two days later, we are back to help with cleaning and putting together beds and cushions. Many students help us. The children who had become refugees twice over in people's houses are now back to settle into their new rooms. Many new students, who have never seen us, arrive this year.

"Hey, do you see Nau Nyaw, Nau Thaw, and Nau Paw?"

"Who? I don't know them".

"Everyone here knows them. They are PaGyi and Moe Htoo's daughters."

"I really don't know them."

"I thought you were helping them yesterday."

"I thought I was helping some Thai ladies from Chaingmai. PaGyi hired some Thai ladies to help us set up new rooms for visitors."

"They are not Thai ladies from Chiangmai. They are Nau Nyaw, Nau Thaw, Nau Paw. Moemoe asked me to call them for dinner. If you see them, let me know."

Housekeeping in Canada has equipped us to do some cleaning and arranging rooms for visitors back home. We are thrilled to help set up rooms for our constant visitors.

—— *Free Burma Ranger (FBR) Courageous Award* ——

On March 28, 2013, one of our volunteer teachers from Nagaland posts a picture of Papa and Moemoe on her facebook page. On her post, I see Dave Eubank, founder of FBR, with his older daughter standing beside him, reading an award for Papa; they are both wearing Free Burma Ranger T-shirts. Papa and Moemoe stand humbly facing the people of Maela. Along with the picture, my Naga friend titles the occasion, Mr. and Mrs. Simon Receiving Award for bravery from Free Burma Rangers.

—— *Global Karen Baptist Fellowship (GKBF)* —— *Courageous Award to Rev. Dr. Simon*

Global Karen Baptist Fellowship has given Papa the Courageous Award at GKBF annual meeting. One of my friends ratifies this award ceremony through messaging.

"Nyaw, how is Canada? Still snowing? I saw your dad at GKBF meeting."

"No more snow in Penticton but still cold. I am glad you saw my dad. How is he?"

"Tired but very well put together. He walks up to receive the award with dignity and shows no need to feel sorry for him. As always, he says God is doing great things in His own time."

"Thanks for letting me know. I need to go to Orange Julius now."

—— *Thra Kennedy and the Builders at Karenni Camp 2* ——

News spread again that there is another big fire at Karenni refugee camp 2. It happens on March 22, 2013. Papa gets a call from his spiritual son at Karenni camp 2 that there is a fire that killed 39 people. Papa needs help from Thra Kennedy. Papa asks a student to go to Thra Kennedy who lives in zone B.

"Hi, come in Thara (sir in Karen). Is there any news? You come all the way here".

"Yes, PaGyi ask me to come to you. Wonder if you can help rebuild some of the buildings in Karenni camp 2."

"Of course, any time."

Soon, Papa arranges a trip for our five construction workers who will volunteer in rebuilding the camp. From Maela refugee camp to Karenni refugee camp 2, it takes nine hours to drive. They will stay in the camp for a month and within a month, they will try to finish the building as much as they can.

First, they build coffins and made 39 graves for the thirty-nine people including one pregnant woman that passed away at the fire. They put their names and UNHCR numbers on the graves. After the burials, they rebuild Karenni Bible School and a church within a month and a half.

On leaving, they are given three Terkunya (wild meat) in a bag as a gift. On their way back, Thai police arrest them for carrying wild meat illegally, plus they don't have Thai Identity cards. Jerry and Papa come to their rescue right away.

"What can we do to avoid them going to prison?"

"We can give them a fine of 300,000.00 Thai baht."

"We will give the money. These are our volunteers who give their time and strength for rebuilding. We will try our best so they will not be in prison."

Then Papa looks at our five volunteers and says, "It is illegal to carry wild animal meat around. Hope you learn the lesson from this."

It is hard to hear the truth. Every fifteen days, they need to go to police station to report. That carries on for a few months until they are completely free. Thara Kennedy is a dedicated pastor who recalls this incident vividly and grateful for Papa's help.

— *2013 A Thinner Papa* —

After spending many sleepless nights in rebuilding, Papa looks thinner than ever. He is tired at the school dedication. He looks tired at Sunday services and 6.00 pm prayer devotion at church. He looks thin and weak. Then someone suggests he should see a doctor.

"I want you to have a full medical checkup at a hospital here."

"I think I will be fine."

"Please come and we will arrange your appointment."

After some weeks, Papa went to see a doctor and comes home with tons of medication. He is diagnosed with TB suspicions.

Meanwhile in Canada, I see his picture.

"Hey Thaw, look at a picture of Papa. Jerry sends me."

"Where? He looks thin and weak. Want to ask Jerry?"

"Hi Jerry, thanks for the picture but PaGyi looks really under the weather."

"I don't know what to say. I just send you the picture," replied Jerry.

"Ok. I will talk to Moemoe," I told Thaw. "Thaw, is your phone card gone?"

"Not yet. 30 minutes left. Here."

"Hello, Moemoe. Papa looks weak. Is he ok?"

"We give him what the doctor gives him. We should stop his medication, maybe."

"If it is TB, don't stop the medication because we are given the medication as well."

"We don't understand. He is not getting any better. He is so weak he cannot even move."

— *2014 November, Chaingmai* —

This time, we fly to Chiangmai to see our parents waiting for us on a bench at the airport. Papa looks weak but he hugs all us with a happy face. Laurie Minuk, our counsellor at Okanagan College, who is loved by all three of us, visits Thailand as well. Papa is very grateful to Thramu Laurie for accompanying us on her visit. Papa has heard about Sir Ben who teaches Thaw how to drive, and Laurie our counsellor since we tell him about them on the phone. He welcomes her and shares his journey with her some evenings when they get some free time.

"Papa, how are you feeling?"

"Doctor says I was given the wrong diagnosis from a previous hospital, so I am hospitalized here in Chaingmai to be treated to get better. I only need to regain my strength. Don't worry, Pomugyigyi."

In fact, the hospital tells him he can sue the doctor and the previous hospital for the wrong medication they provide, but Papa chooses not to sue anyone.

"Papa, look at me."

As always, he looks so sweet. He smiles a little looking at my i-style phone. I take his picture.

— *2015 Last Convocation and Thaw and Posi's Wedding* —

March 2015 is the last convocation of KKBBSC that Papa conducts. He gathers all his strength to lead this, his last KKBBSC convocation. A man full of integrity, sincerity, and love. He stands tall and gives a full history of the school, sits down until the convocation ends.

He is trustworthy. He often says this at chapel. "If people cannot trust you, earn their trust. Once they can trust you, do not let them down." Papa lives what he preaches.

After the annual graduation, Papa writes a letter to Htee Ger Nee Baptist Church for Thaw and Posi's (Saw Blut Soe) wedding. The wedding is going to happen on April 21, 2015. Thaw and Posi choose that date because Posi's parents married on April 20 and Moemoe and Papa got married on April 22. They choose a day between their parents' wedding. It is a great occasion as both families are coming to celebrate a wonderful day.

Papa is very weak, but he officiates the wedding until it ends. His middle daughter is now married. Paw and I are still singles. He has no appetite to take pictures with anyone as his time and energy are overtaxed. Meanwhile, when he gets home, he poops on his red tehgu and the waste is all over the front of the toilet.

"Papa, why don't you wear adult diaper?"

"No need, Pomugyi."

"Papa, but if you need you should."

He is smiling and said nothing back. I am wiping his waste in front of the toilet, chiding my Papa immaturely.

— *The Second Fall, April 25, 2015* —

On April 24, 2015, the whole family comes to Chaingmai, we will go back to Canada, Posi's family will go to USA, and Papa will go to the hospital for a follow-up checkup. Everyone is busy that night. We go shopping with Posi's family and come home late. In the morning, Papa is in the washroom, cleaning himself. He disappears too long so I call Moemoe. "Moemoe, please ask Papa if he needs help."

"Eh Lay, are you okay?"

"I fell."

"Nyaw, open the door."

"I cannot. Papa locks it."

"Eh Lay, why do you lock the door?"

Papa does not give us any reply. He crawls slowly to the door and unlocks it. The three minutes that he crawls seems like an hour for us who waits anxiously at the door. He finally comes out and we all cry. We repent for not sitting beside him that night. I regret. I repent. I cry. We cry on our way to the airport, while Moemoe and Papa are leaving for the hospital.

By the time we arrive Canada, Moemoe sent the news that Papa must go through an operation. He broke his leg from the fall. Doctors find out he has stage four liver cancer. Moemoe says this to encourage us.

Doctors speak in front of our friends and family who come to visit that day. After he announces Papa's diagnosis, Thra Wado gathers everyone to surround Papa and pray for him. Both Papa and I are calm. We leave all in God's hands. Doctors hold a two hour meeting on how best to help Papa. They said, they have heard a lot about him. Because he has impacted many lives, they want to take good care of him. Although he has no Identity card nor any legal paper, they put him in a VIP room to take care of him, and he is visited by the head Doctor and head nurse. Do not worry. God will take care of us.

—— *Visitors verses Privacy* ——

Many visitors visit Papa. His Korean friends fly in just to visit him. Dr Frank Green visits him. Many people pay a visit to him. Doctors suggest anyone who visit need to wash their hands before they touch him. Papa heeds that in his heart. He turns to me and says this.

"Pomugyi, when Thaw and Posi come, remind them to wash their hands before they come in."

"Yes, Papa. I will remind them."

I turn my head around and cry because it is impossible for Thaw to come back as she is in her first trimester of pregnancy and has been suggested to rest. Paw returns the next week from Canada.

Many visitors visit everyday until Papa gets tired of speaking. As days go on, he no longer can make the effort to speak about KKBC, KKBBSC, churches, Global Karen Baptist Fellowship and any ministry related issues. All he cares about and all we care is if he poops today. What is his sugar level, and can he finish his meal or not? We measure his blood pressure everyday and all we care about is if he is feeling alright.

—— *The Very Last Three Months* ——

Today is 16 July 2015. Papa still has a very good memory. Today, he points his fingers to me signaling text reading time. I reach out to read his messages and the news from the Thai newspaper, The Nation. He listens carefully as I read out one world news report after another. He even corrects my English when I pronounce incorrectly. For example, present and presentation. At times, his speech is nonsensical,

"Pomugyi, I have already sent a message, but people blocked them. Why do they block it?"

"Dayee, go let the nurse know Papa wants to take shower in the washroom. He wants to clean himself and gets cool off."

Dayee disappeared and came back with two nurses.

"Does the patient need to shower?"

Papa – "Poetu, do you leave me here to die?"

Nyaw – "Papa, please do not say that. What do you want?"

Papa – "Want to cool off in the washroom. Bring me Jerry's sandals."

"Jerry is home. He has not come."

"Then bring me Teeradet's sandals."

"Teeradet is in Maela camp."

"Bring me a pair of heavy good sandals. I will clean myself in the washroom."

"Can you handle that? Your blood pressure is pretty low 87/51 today."

"Ohhhhhh"

His 'Ohhh' is very pitiful but every time he said 'Ohhhhh', we smile because it is somehow comforting. It is a very cute sound. Moemoe calls Dayee and arranges a cold shower with the nurses in the bathroom. They take off Papa's clothes and pour some cups of water on him. He feels better. He feels fresh. It shows on his face when he comes out of the bathroom.

"Papa" (Smiling at Papa)

"Pomugyi, go and check the fresh air."

"Ok."

Sometimes I go out to check sometimes I don't. I cry outside and come back.

"It is still hot, Papa. The temperature is 20 Celsius plus. Too hot for you, Papa."

Papa is a little disappointed, but he seems alright.

"Pomugyi, go and check fresh air."

"Ok, Papa."

"Is it cool now?"

"Yes, Papa. Tonight, the air is cool."

"I want to have fresh air."

"Dayee, let's take Papa outside. Do you need to call a nurse to help you? I feel nervous whenever you carry Papa."

"I will be fine, Nau."

"You sure? Very sure?"

Dayee does not give any reply. He helps Papa dress and puts him in a wheel chair. Then we are off outside.

Today, we are off outside. Jerry is back. Jerry takes three pictures for us. None of us says anything. I hug Papa. I hold his right ear. I always feel a little envious every time Paw touches Papa's ears. I wish to hold his ear too but did not have a chance to hold it. Now, I hold it and feel good. Papa turns to face me and says, "You can hold both my ears." I touch his ears, and I am touched. I weep.

"Pomugyi, will you get a visa from the Foundation?"

"I don't know, Papa. Let's leave everything in God's hands. If I get a work permit, I can have a bank account, then I can work legally in

Thailand. I can teach at KKBBSC. If I get, I get, if I don't, I don't. I am not worried."

Papa looks quiet disapproval of what he hears. "If you will be a blessing for others, do it, for the good of others. Don't give up."

—— *Never Give Up* ——

At night.

"Pomugyi, help me count how many times I move my feet."

"One, two, three… seven, eight, nine, ten."

"Let me rest a little, Pomugyi."

After moving his feet for a thousand times, he is tired and falls asleep.

In the daytime, Papa is given a spirometer to blow into to help strengthen his lungs. He blows into the device a hundred times each day.

"Pomugyi, when will you get married? It is time to think about that."

"I love someone, but it is complicated."

Papa turns his head to indicate he does not want to hear excuses. Moemoe encourages Papa to live to see Paw and I get married. Everyday, Papa is fighting every second to live.

—— *The Coziness of Family* ——

At night, we return to a place where we sleep. It costs us a rent of eight thousand baht per month (we live there for almost two months). This space enables Papa to be surrounded by Paw, Dayee, Jerry, Teeradet, Moemoe and me. Papa makes sure that we are not buying but renting while he is unhealthy. The house is not ours; it is rented. Our house is in Maela refugee camp. While I am giving someone an address of the house.

"Pomugyi, are you saying that we are renting this home only, not buying?"

"Yes, I told him we are renting. This is not our house."

Papa feels cozy when he is surrounded by loved ones. At night, no one speaks a word. Everyone is praying, and everyone is singing. Deep down, everyone knows that the time is near. Everyone sings a song "Nearer to Thee, O Lord," with tears pouring inside.

—— *Hallucination* ——

"Po Tu, if you can just cooperate, we will be done building by now."

Moemoe thinks "no way, that is crazy people's works. I am not participating."

"Ok. Po Dah put up your hands. Straight. That is right. Both hands. Po Dah stands there for a few minutes. Don't move."

"You go on the other side. Ok. There. Straight."

"Good. That is a triangle."

While they are standing for almost half an hour, Teeradet is videotaping the scene. He is laughing very hard until he is chided by Moemoe.

"Don't laugh, Teeradet. I am not laughing. This is not something to laugh about."

Papa sees Teeradet.

"Come, Teeradet. Come here. Straighten your hand. No, not like that. The other side of Po Dah. Ok. Good. Now, we have a square building."

Teeradet stands up and expresses "oh, no. How many hours should I stand here?"

"There move a little to that side, Po Tu."

"Eh Lay, are you done? Hurry up."

"Po Tu, very nice."

For Papa, this building should be perfectly square.

"Moemoe, shouldn't we let his doctor know?"

"Call her, Po Dah."

"Who knows her number? Ok. I get it. I will call her."

"Hello, Maw (Doctor in Thai)? Please come to see with your own eyes what happened to my dad now. He asked us to build buildings with our hands. He does not allow us to sleep. We have been standing for three hours now."

"When did it happen?"

"Since ten or eleven."

"Ok. I am coming now."

"Eh Lay, doctor is at the door."

"Oh, Thramu, come in."

Everyone puts their hands down and ready for bed. While they have a minute to relax, the doctor speaks to them.

Why do you listen to Dr. Simon's hallucination? He is fantasizing because some of his organs are no longer working. With the heavy drugs that they give him at the hospital, he is now hallucinating. This happened because his liver is not working. No need to please a patient.

Momoe softly answers.

"So hard not to please him as he is a wonderful leader that everyone listens to. We love him, respect him, and want to make him happy. He has done so much for us."

"I understand, Thramu. But if you please him every night, you will get sick too."

— Music —

During his last few months, Papa asks to listen to To Kee Po and Pu Ba Tin's music only. He keeps asking for that music. I request my best friend Kay Nay Ywa to download the music.

"Hi Pokay. Can you help me download To Kee Po and Pu Ba Tin's music for PaGyi?"

"Paw told me about that. They are in your memory stick."

"You already download it?"

"Check your computer and memory stick."

"Ok. Thank you."

"No need to thank me. Please take care of Pagyi. Nyi."

"I don't know what to do for Papa during this time. You have gone through this before."

"When you look at him, smile. That will give him strength to face the world."

— *Teeradet and the Password* —

Since Teeradet has many sleepless nights, Jerry will replace him soon.

Teeradet must be very tired. He leaves as soon as Jerry arrives. Teeradet leaves WiFi password for Jerry.

"Po Dah, where is the thing you carry every night? They are beside you. A red thing."

"A red thing, Papa? Oh, my tablet."

"Yes, give it to me."

"Let's listen to your favorite music na. Pu Ba Tin or To Kee Po?"

"No, not tonight."

"What do you want, Papa?"

Papa holds the tablet with both hands and speaks very loudly, "Teeradet, where are you? Teeradet? Password? Teeradet?" Looking at Papa's hallucination, I am crying.

"Nyaw, don't cry. Not good for Papa to see you cry."

"I am trying, Pawpi, I feel like I am slowly losing my Papa.

— *Carry the Pain* —

We are taking Papa for a walk – Dayee, Paw, Moemoe and me. Papa is thirsty, so I give him water. While he is drinking, he is bleeding. We quickly take him back. At night, he asks me to take his feet up and down for exercise. I see him look up and stare at the ceiling. After a few hours, we realize Papa is unconscious. We take him to the emergency. After some minutes, Papa regains consciousness. I am waiting outside ICU. Nurses give me a signal that I can enter now. I go in and hold his hands, "Papa, is it very painful." He nods. "very painful". I weep.

—— *Different Prayers* ——

"We pray that Papa will get better soon."

"I know, Thaw Thi. Let me tell you the truth. Papa is getting weaker every day. His day is coming to an end."

"Have a little faith, Nyaw."

"Thaw, for me, having faith is more than believing in physical healing. Having faith means surrendering to God no matter what happens".

"Nyaw, when I talk to Moemoe, she told me Papa is getting better everyday."

"That is what Moemoe wishes, Thaw Thi. The truth is…"

"Ok. I don't want to hear bad news. I am crying every day."

"We cry too. It is very hard to face."

During these few months, some people ask God to heal Papa. Even in our little family, Moemoe and Thaw believe Papa will get better. Paw and I, on the contrary, think Papa is going home soon. The tension during this time is very high. It is so hard even to answer a phone call.

—— *Facebook Posts* ——

Papa is in bed. He cannot move, but he moves us profoundly. He asked us to buy KFC for the doctors and nurses who look after him. He asks us to buy a cake for Moemoe on her birthday.

June 22, 2015. Moemoe is 24/7 with the love of her life since he became unwell last year. She doesn't complain about her pain or think of her own sickness. Praying constantly, I call her a godly woman of substance. My hero, my mom, I love you. Happy birthday, Moemoe.

Papa asks me to post this because many people think highly of him and pressure him to live. For me, this is all he leaves for me. This post is my inheritace – TO PUT GOD FIRST.

June 17, 2015. Dear friends, Papa (my dad) wants me to thank everyone here for your love for him. Thanks for your concern, help and constant prayers. He also reminds us to give God the first place in our lives and remember not to think highly of his position (my dad as a leader). To God alone, we give glory. Blessings and much love, Nyaw.

By the end of July, someone posts a picture of Papa in bed. Before I have a chance to speak to him, Thaw, who lives in Dallas has already seen the picture. In response to his posts, she writes this.

> Please, if any one happened to visit my father, please please please don't take photos and share it on facebook. It is already painful not to be able to be with my dad as soon as I want to… it is like killing me… thanks. Prayers is all I need.

— *August 2, 2015 Farewell* —

People of Maela refugee camp who live close by are gathering to welcome him back. Some think Papa is getting better. Some think he will stay in the camp for a few months still. Moemoe who always prays and hopes for Papa's recovery has recently talked to our Thai Karen pastors in Chiangmai about his potential grave.

"Yes, Thradoh, what will happen if he passes away in Chiangmai?"

"We have a very peaceful cemetery for Christians here in Chaingmai. His foreigner friends can come easily for his funeral. Our TKBC community here can do a celebration of his life here."

"I see. That means refugees and displaced people cannot attend his funeral if he passes away here. I will ask my daughters to speak to the doctors to discuss this."

"We talk to Thai doctors at Suandok (Maharaj Nakorn Chaingmai hospital). They said it will be hard to take him back to the camp if he dies in Chiang Mai because he has no identity card."

"Our advice is if you want him to finish in the camp, you better take him while he is breathing due to his status as a man with no ID."

August 1st, early. Moemoe calls us to her side.

Paw, you and Polerm go with the hospital ambulance with Papa. Jerry, Nyaw and I will pack everything up and go home early. We must go today. Doctors suggest we do it as soon as possible.

Moemoe, Jerry, and I arrive Maela around 7.00 pm. The ambulance has not shown up yet.

"Paw, where are you now?"

"We are still on the way. Arrived Tak".

Some time later,

"Moemoe, Papa is breathing slower now. He breaths every ten seconds."

"You are brave, Podah. We are praying for you. Update me when you can."

August 2nd, 4.00 a.m. Paw makes her final call to Moemoe.

"Moemoe, we just passed into Zone A, Papa has stopped breathing."

In 1990, Papa enters Maela refugee camp as a displaced person. Twenty-five years later, the ambulance drops him off and leaves him in the camp without documenting his passing away. He lives in Maela as a man with no Identity for twenty-five years. Then he passes away with no identity. Papa is a true displaced person.

— *Papa's Good Works that Benefits His Remaining Children* —

Eh Naung Soe's Wedding is February 16, 2019. We are stopped at the front Thai gate two times. Finally, we head to Maesod, cross to Myawaddy and to the wedding. After the wedding, we cross the river to Maesod.

"Stop there, you guys. Do you have any paper to travel?"

"Yes, we do."

"The driver hands Thai police a letter. He looks around and said."

"You have no identities. You should not travel like this. This is illegal in Thailand."

Everyone is quiet. This is fate of refugees. Looks like we will need to go to jail.

"Where are you heading to?"

"Maela refugee camp."

"Maela? Which section?"

"Zone C. C1A. KKBBSC. Bible College."

"Ajarn Simon's school?"

"Yes. We are from Dr. Simon's school."

"Is he well? Say hi to him for me. I know him."

"He passed away… err… almost four years now."

"Oh, I didn't know that. If you are from Ajarn Simon school, you are free to go. Next time, ask permission from your camp commander. For now, you can go."

<u>The following is the exact record of Pagyi Rev. Dr. Simon to the questions presented him in an interview conducted by Dr. Saw Wado on August 6th, 2014</u>

Name and Personal Detail: Saw Simon, 64 years old, born in Naung Bo Village, 1949 (the year also saw the birth of Karen Revolution), 19 July (the day General Aung San assassinated) Pagu Division), Karen State; he has seven siblings, two of them passed away; married to Thra Mu Tablut Htoo and they have three daughters currently living and studying in Canada.

Education: He received his primary education from Naung Bo and Hsa Bu Taung Village, matriculated in the town of Ler Doh in 1969. He did his B.Th and B.D. Myanmar Institute of Theology, Insein, Yangon. Went to the Philippines in 1985 for his M.Th degree. Awarded Doctor of Divinity degree by the ABGTS in 1998.

Leadership Position: He is currently serving as the principal of Kawthoolei Karen Baptist Bible School and Collage (1989-current), general secretary of Kawthoolei Karen Baptist Churches (1989-current), Chair of the Global Karen Baptist Fellowship (2014-current). He is also the recipient of the BWA's Human Rights Award, 2000 and Global Karen Baptist's Mission Imminent Award 2013.

Key Statement: "I see the future of our people as very positive. We have raised many young and visionary leaders to lead the next generation; they are now spreading all over the world: in Europe, America, Australia, including Thai Karen hills. They are taking leadership responsibilities in churches in many different parts of the world. We have hope; God is using our people in a very special way. Young leaders like Thra Teetoh,

Thra Wado, Thra Peacefully, Thra Hsa Lershee, Rev. Htoo Gay, Rev. Htoo Wah. They have a shared vision to renew, rebuild and restore our national identity and our community in Kawthoolei, I support them wholeheartedly in their endeavor to implement that dream."

Trauma and Exilic Experience: I was brought up in extreme poverty. My parents cannot support my education. My aunts in Ler Doh support my school education. When I graduated from high school in 1969, I wanted to join the arts, and science - college but God turned me in a different direction.

During vacation, I participated in Pagu's division sports and games competitions. I participated in a lot of events. One day I came back, I had difficulty to breathe. Then, Dr. Sein, the Indian doctor, he pushed my chest and asked me to breathe, he repeated the pushing for a few times and told me to rest. "You are over exercised," he told me. I was hospitalized for some days. While I was in hospital I prayed to God, "If you let me live through this ordeal and let me live, I will go to Bible school and become your minister." I was interested in joining the freedom Karen fighter movement and fight for the freedom of my people. I wanted to be an army general. God saw what I did not see, I got sick and things turned around for me in a different direction.

The first twenty years of my life were spent in studies in primary and secondary education. I matriculated by 1969 in Ler Doh high school. The next twenty years (from 1969-19889) was spent in theological education and as teacher of theology in Karen Baptist Theological Seminary in Insein, Rangoon. In 1985 I went to the Philippines forfurther studies and came back in 1987.

In 1988, there was a big uprising in Burma. It is called the 8.8.88 uprising. There were killings; we heard gunfire days and nights, thousands of people died when the military cracked down on pro-democracy protesters. There were also rumors the army will put poison in water supplies and in food. In some instances, the actually did. There were rumors some yellow cars would come drop poison into the wells and water supplies. People become apprehensive with the sight of every yellow car. The army ran the country by inflicting fear. The people panicked. On top of that the army released criminal inmates from the Insein prison to instigate trouble. They were given a pack of rice and 20 Kyats each to go around beating up the protesters. There was looting and lawlessness everywhere in the city of Rangoon. We also heard gunfire in Insein prison. To accommodate more prisoners in Insein prison, the army shot prisoners to clear out rooms for the incoming prisoners—the protestors. The white bridge in near inya lake in Rangoon had become a red bridge when the army shot students, monks and protesters on that bridge. There were army tanks everywhere in the city and because of the tanks roads were destroyed.

We did not want to stay in Rangoon anymore. My wife did not want to stay there anymore. So we came up to the Border to serve my people. I have always wanted to serve my people by the border. By 1988, August, there was an army crackdown in Burma. Rangoon was in turmoil. So the 88's uprising opened up a rare opportunity for me and my family to come to Thai-Burma border.

"The next set of 20, (from 1989 onwards) years of my life is being spent by Thai Burma border and in the refugee camp of Thailand where I serve my people as theological educator and secretary general of KKBC. It is wonderful how God uses me to serve my people in the refugee camps along Thai-Burma border here to prepare the next generation for mission, evangelism of the world and for the next line up leadership for our people. We are grateful to God for everything.

"By October 1989, I was elected the principal of the Kawthoolei Karen Baptist Bible School and General Secretary of Kawthoolei Karen Baptist Churches. I was elected principal of a school without teachers and without students. By the end of 1989, Gaw Lay was attacked and later abandoned. We had to run to the Thai side of the border. We finally moved to Maela camp in 1990 where we had to rebuild the school from scratch in Maela Camp.

"Again in April 2012, the School burned down to ashes again here in Maela Camp. Nothing was left. But we rebuilt the school this time with better materials, bigger than before and stronger than the previous one. God can do anything.

Future Hope: "God is doing great things in my life. I see the future of our people as very positive. We have raised many young and visionary leaders to lead the next generation; they are now spreading all over the world: in Europe, America, Australia, including Thai Karen hills. They are taking leadership responsibilities in churches in many different parts of the world. God is using our people in a very special way. We have hope God will do new things in the future."

Kawthoolei Karen Baptist Bible School & College P.O. Box 11, Mae Sot, Tak 63110. Thailand. Email: simon2_ kkbc@yahoo.com or simon2kkbc@gmail.com

Sunday, August 04, 2013

Dear brothers and sisters in Christ, this is my short testimony of how God is so good and so faithful in fulfilling His promises to all His loving children irrespective of time and space, tongue and race, faith and belief, age and sex, geography and nationality, rich and poor, educated and uneducated. God gave me a dream and He is fulfilling it step by step. I was born on Tuesday, July 19 (the day Gen. Aung San and many of his cabinet members were assassinated), 1949(the year the Karen started their struggle for justice, rights and freedom) and grew up in a Christian family in a village called NaungBoh, in Kawa township, Pegu/Pago division. After finishing my primary school education in my village, I wanted very much to pursue for higher education, but my parents could not afford sending me to school. But praise the Lord they allowed me to leave the village to continue my further education. Before leaving the village, God gave me a very wonderful dream, which I dreamt it for three consecutive nights. It was March 1963, one year after Gen. Ne Win led a military coup and took the power from U Nu, the then Prime Minister of Burma and established the military rule in Burma. I dreamt that I was flying in the air, over the seas, over the mountains, and over the valley, like a superman, free of worry and fear. Look at how God fulfill my dream. I left my village and went to stay with my uncle and aunt (cousin of my mother) family in a village near LehGu, called Sabudaung and studied there from 1963 to 1966 and finished my 7th grade there. Then I went to Kyauk-kyi and stayed with my aunt (a twin sister of my mother) family from 1966 to 1969 and finished my High School Final (10th Grade) in Science. Then I joined the Burma Divinity School (BDS), name changed toBurma Institute of Theology (BIT) when the Golden Jubilee was celebrated in 1974 and now to Myanmar Institute of Theology (MIT). First I did the B.Th. program and then B.D. program and was called to join the BIT as one of the professors. I got married with Thramu Ta BlutHtoo, the eldest daughter of the late Brigadier Johnny Htoo of the 6th Brigade of the Karen National Liberation Army (1949 to 1963) and the Rev. Johnny Htoo, pastor of Taunggyi Karen Baptist Church (1967 to 1989)and Mrs. Starry Johnny Htoo on April 22, 1980, during the joint meeting of the Karen Baptist Convention and the Upper Burma Karen Baptist Churches Association in Kalaw(it was a triple wedding attended by more than a thousand people) and blessed with three daughters, Nyaw, Thaw and Paw (now all study and live in Canada). I was sent to the Philippines to do my Master and then Doctoral studies as the staff development program of the BIT/MIT at the Asia Baptist Graduate Theological Seminary (ABGTS) from 1985 to 1987 and with my own eyes witnessed the People Power Movement of the power struggle between Corazon Aquino and Marcos. I came back to Burma in June 1987 and continued my teaching at the BIT/MIT and as all of us knew, the uprising / people power movement / the 8.8.88 demonstration that led to another military coup by Gen. Saw Maung resulting from the closure of all the schools, universities, colleges, and all Bible Schools and Seminaries. I then decided to come to the Karen State, Kawthoolei to be with my suffering people and serve God through serving my poor and needy and suffering Karen people and left Rangoon in March 1989. There were lots of difficulties and hardships but God enabled me to fly over all of them. I was elected to serve the Lord as the Principal of the Kawthoolei Karen Baptist Bible School and College and the Secretary of the Kawthoolei Karen Baptist Churches since 1990at the KKBC Annual Mass Meeting held in October, 1989 at TavoyMergui Area of Churches Association. We went through **war:**we had to leave Wallei, our village where we have our KKBBSC located and move to Maela camp in March, 1990. As I said I was elected as the new Principal of the KKBBSC during the Annual Meeting of the KKBC in October 1989 held in TavoyMergui Area of Churches Association and became the newly elected Principal of the KKBBSC without school buildings and teachers and students when Wallei was occupied by the Burma Army. We then prayed and rebuilt and started our ministry of teaching and equipping in Maela camp in June, 1990. DKBA attacked the camp in February 1996 killing two grandmothers, **flood:**-there was a great flood that destroyed our kitchen and the Church on September 24, 1996 and then the **fire:** that torched to ashes all the KKBBSC buildings in the compound on April 28, 2012. In all these things and critical and difficult times God gave me no fear and no worry. Like Ps. 66:12 said, "We went through fire and through water; yet you have brought us out to a spacious place." I have no fear and no worry when leaving Walleiin December 1989 when all the school buildings were burnt by the Burma Army and when the DKBA attacked the camp in February 1996, no fear and no worry when a great flood destroyed our kitchen and church on September 24, 1996, no fear and no worry when all the buildings were torched to ashes by fire on April 28, 2012 and without hesitation gave all the iron bars of all the buildings destroyed by the fire to the camp Commander (2 big truck loads and 3 pickup truck loads) when he asked for, because I am strongly convinced that God will provide all that we need and give us everything new in His time and for His glory. God is so good and so faithful in fulfilling His promises. Come, visit, and see and witness with your own eyes what the Lord has done, is doing and will be doing for us all in His own time and for His glory. Thank you all so much for helping us in ways and means you can as with our hands we rebuild our buildings. God's new gifts are bigger, wider, stronger, greater and better. This gives us a new vision and new insight of always growing bigger, wider, stronger, greater and better in the ministry of serving the Lord through serving His suffering people. Our KKBBSC which started with only 4 teachers and 6 students now growing from one Program to 2 Programs with 36 faculty and staff (including 6 studying abroad)as coworkers in serving the Lord in this wonderful teaching and equipping ministry and 451 students studying in the two programs. By the grace of God we were able to have our KKBC Annual Mass Meeting from April 9 to 13,2013 followed by the Graduation Exercises of our KKBBSC on Sunday, April 14, 2013, 2 pm with 58 students graduated from the KKBBSC. By the grace of God we reopened our KKBBSC for the academic year 2013-2014 on June 9th 2013 with close to five hundred students enrolled. Praise the Lord. We would like to humbly request you all to come, visit, encourage and see with your eyes what the Lord has done for us, is doing for us and what He will do for us. God bless you all. The followings are some of the poems I composed as the Lord led me to fly across and over the seas, the mountains, and the valley.

<u>Our Living Testimony - 1</u>

They call us a displaced people, But praise God we are not misplaced. They say they see no hope for our future, But praise God our future is as bright as the promises of God. They see they say the life of our people is a misery, But praise God our life is a mystery. For what they say is what they see, And what they see is temporal, But ours is the eternal. All because we put our self, In the hands of God we trust.

<u>Our Living Testimony - 2</u>

We lost everything with the fire that caught on our KKBBSC on April 28,2012, but we still have everything, because God is our Everything.

Gone with the fire are our sins and transgressions, not His mercy and Grace.

Gone with the fire are the buildings and material things that can be replaced even with the better ones, but praise God, no life was lost.

Gone with the fire are the 4 visitors' Note that contained best wishes, prayers, encouragements and promises by friends around the world, but not their continuing love, care and concern for us expressed in their words and deeds.

Gone with the fire are our fears and doubts, not our faith in the Almighty and living God. Rev. Dr. Saw Simon, Principal, KKBBSC, Maela Camp. April 28,2012.

I AM NOT ASHAMED TO BE A REFUGEE

I am not ashamed to be a refugee, for I know my Lord, my Master, my Saviour was a refugee long long before me.

I am not afraid to be a refugee, for though I am displaced, I am not misplaced.

I will never feel lonely, for God gives me many friends around the world.

I will never feel helpless, for God gives me many hands for help.

I will never stop doing good things in spite of all the difficulties and hardships, for I know that this is the real purpose of life God has entrusted to each one of us.

I will never feel regret being a refugee, for though life is full of limitations, restrictions and tragedies, it is enriched with meanings and values.

I will never feel hopeless, for my Saviour promised me an eternal home in heaven.

I will never plan for a revenge, for vengeance is mine, I will repay, says the Lord, the only Just and Judge of all.

I am glad to be a refugee, for I am always reminded that my eternal home is in heaven and not on this earth.

But I know that for the time being, Satan is trying to enslave me, for though I live in my Father's, my brothers' and sisters' world, I am not free to travel.

However, I am strongly convinced that a day will come and it will be soon that I will be able to travel freely to visit my brothers and sisters around the world and say "Thank you" for what they have done.

I will then see the beauty of my Father's world. Amen.

I wander as I wonder.

I wander as I wonder,
On life's journey as refugee,
Away from home and dear loved ones,
All the news read and received,
All the news I heard and seen,
Full of untold miseries:
People killed and being killed,
People raped and being raped,
People oppressed and being oppressed,
People sold and being sold,
People held and being held,
And detained in many ways:

Imprisoned, jailed and house arrest.
But -
When I turned to God in prayers,

And I read His Holy Word,
Then I wonder as I wander,
A child of God on life's journey

Nearer home and all loved ones,
All the pages turned and read,
All messages heard and seen,
full of unfolding mysteries:
People loved and being loved,
People helped and being helped,

Kind people showing kindness,
Following the Master's steps,
What had happened here on earth,
Fulfilling His Holy Word,

He is coming very soon,
Let us be watchful and ready.

Thank you and God bless you all. Sincerely yours in the ministry of the Lord among the displaced Karen people in the camps and the Internally Displaced Areas,

(Rev. Dr. Saw Simon)
Principal
KKBBSC
Mae La Camp.

144

ကီၢ်သူလ့ၤကညီဘျၢထံခရံာ်ဖိလံာ်စီဆှံကၠိဒီးခီလ့ၣ်ကွံ

KAWTHOOLEI KAREN BAPTIST BIBLE SCHOOL & COLLEGE
P.O. BOX 11, MAE SOT, TAK 63110, THAILAND.
Mobile Pho. 0810397794. E-mail: simon2_kkbc@yahoo.com

Friday, April 27, 2012

ကညီဖိဖၢၣ်ဒုၣ်ဒွဲၣ်-ဒုၣ်ဒွဲၣ်လၢလ့ၤဒိၣ်အပူၤ.

To Whom It May Concern:

Subject: Letter of Recommendation & Requesting for necessary help and
             assistance for traveling.

Love, Peace, Justice = Unity & Blessings.

Dear Sir or Madam;

        We are going to Noh Poe camp to attend the wedding to be held there on Saturday, April 28, 2012. We have been living and serving the Lord in the camps for more than 22 years and we thank the Royal Family, especially His Majesty the King & Her Majesty the Queen, the Royal Thai Government, the Authorities concerned and the people of Thailand for allowing us to take refuge in the Kingdom on humanitarian bases and together with the UNHCR, the NGOs and churches and individuals for providing needs for our protection, our survival and ministry. We would be very much grateful if the authorities concerned could kindly provide any necessary help and assistance needed as we travel. Your kindness and kind assistance will be greatly appreciated and remembered by all of us. May God shower His bountiful blessings upon each and every one of you.

S.n	Name	Age	Sex	H. No.	UN-MOI Reg. #	Remark
1.	Rev. Dr. Saw Simon	62	M	C1A – 157	MLA020361	Principal
2.	Thramu Ta Blut Htoo Simon	62	F	C1A – 157	MLA020361	Teacher

"Let us not grow weary while doing good, for in due season we shall reap if we do not lose heart. Galatians 6:9."

We love HM the King and we will try our best to live in obedience to his insightful advice: – "Stay honest, minimize prejudice, and strengthen kindness and unity."

In His Service,

(Rev. Dr. Saw Simon)
Principal
KKBBSC
Mae La Camp

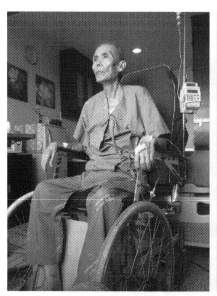
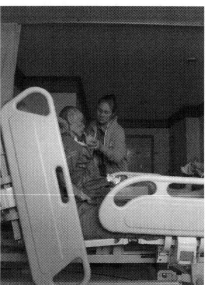

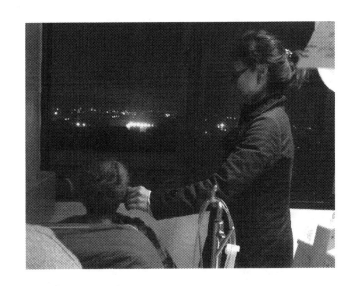

Printed in the United States
By Bookmasters